Contents

CHAPTER 1

The Seven Spells Of A Turbo Transformation

By Jon Le Tocq

"Jon, I'm going on holiday soon. If my wife see's me like this in a pair of shorts on the beach, she may well call the coastguard. You've got three weeks to get me into them, which I guess are 3-4 inches too small right now."

I kid you not, these are the exact words used by a client of mine who we will refer to as Miserable Big Dave, and it coincided with a conversation I had with a friend of mine who is also a leading fat loss expert.

This discussion would best be summarized as "Why the **** do people always leave it so late. What's the best you can do in 21 days?"

I'm going to tell you the seven things I got Dave to do, but first let me tell you that this was tough...for me!

I've been brought up to believe in hard work and that nothing 'just happens'.

Having developed as a strength and conditioning coach who continues to study the very best training and nutrition methods on the planet, I can state one thing.

You will NOT get the body you want in three weeks.

However, I have also proved beyond doubt on hundreds of people through the birth of the Turbo Transformation program, that you can produce some blinding results in that time.

These are the kinds of results that lead people to accuse you of Photoshopping transformation photos.

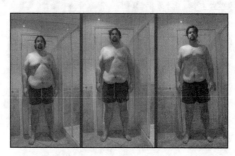

I love when that happens. It means I've achieved MY goal of giving my client results that are beyond most people's comprehension!

Now I want to share the seven key things I stirred together in my famous cauldron to create the fastest working, healthiest, lasting fat loss protocol I've ever designed.

What started off as an experiment without much hope became known as the *Turbo Transformation*. It has been used to great effect by men and women from 18 to 55 (as far as I know) in my home island of Guernsey, England, Scotland, Mexico, the USA, Australia and the Middle East.

I say this not to impress you but to impress upon you that <u>this protocol works for anyone and everyone</u>.

Why?

Because it targets three things:

1. Rebuilding your health and vitality in days

2. Restoring the function of your digestive system which is the keystone in all things fat loss

3. Laser-focused application of simple methods even if you don't have a personal coach physically kicking your butt!

The magic is in the consistency with no margin for if's and but's or excuses.

You have 21 days to get shocking results.

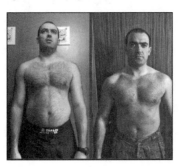

This requires throwing out everything you thought you knew and all the wonderful tips you picked up from know-it-all friends and journalists capable of dramatizing 'amazing new methods' which are actually utter crap and get hung out to dry when the next fad arrives.

Generally I like people to ask questions. It shows I am educating them rather than creating a robotic moron incapable of making decisions when they go out for meals, go on holiday or are faced with choices – of which modern life is crammed full!

However, for now, if you are unsure about the validity or profound effects of the *Seven Spells of the Turbo Transformation,* just try it.

Give me seven days to prove myself and these methods. Again.

1. DRINK 2-3 LITRES OF WATER PER DAY

Water.

I sometimes feel we don't need to talk about this anymore. Surely everyone knows just how important water is by now? Apparently not, as I still hear people say they've not drunk more than one or two cups per day. And one of those was warm and full of caffeine. Entire books have been written on the benefits of water, but let's keep it simple.

Toxins (the ones from all the processed food you keep eating) are stored in your fat cells. If you want your body to feel confident that it can release these fat cells without poisoning your body, you need to put in some magical fluid that will maintain the flow of your bloodstream and flush out these toxins quicker than you can spell detoxification.

No magical fluid means no letting go of fat cells. You need a fluid that constitutes the majority of your brain so that you are able to think more clearly and control stress levels, which play havoc with your hormones and leave you storing fat for fun.

You need a fluid that makes up 70-80% of a healthy muscle, which can function well and cope with the stresses and strains of the exercise you need to do to accelerate fat loss.

You need a fluid which gives structure to your cells – the engine of your body and the little cretins that either utilize fat for fuel or store it depending on the instructions given by your brain.

You need water, and a good dollop of it on a daily basis.

2. CYCLE CARBOHYDRATES

Carbohydrates aren't the enemy that those Calfornian size zero models like to make them out to be. Long-term carbohydrate restriction has been shown to reduce thyroid function, which is what dictates at how fast a rate your metabolism burns. Think of it as your fat burning thermostat.

However, eating carbs all the time as most people do these days, is asking for trouble. Carbs are the easiest fuel to burn for your body – easier to convert to energy than your body fat.

It's like a man lost in the wilderness choosing between a box of match-es and a magnifying glass and some twigs to start a fire. Whilst both will work sooner or later, why take the hard option?

Consequently, if you're always pouring carbs into your body, you will use these for energy requirements, at best leaving your body fat where it is, and at worst, storing even more as the excess sugars are converted to triglycerides and stored as fat.

So what's the solution? Implement carb cycling.

Three or four days of low carb days (vegetables only and maybe some fruit in your post-workout shake) followed by a high carb day to reset the 'thyroid thermostat'.

Rinse and repeat.

You can also strategically throw in regular 24-hour periods of intermittent fasting as we do on the Turbo Transformation program. This accelerates fat loss even more and also gives the digestive system a much needed rest!

3. FOCUS ON INTENSITY NOT DURATION

When it comes to training for fat loss, more is rarely better unless you are currently inactive or go to church more often than you go to the gym.

No session need be more than 60 minutes (including warm up and mobility):

• Warm up and mobility: 10-15 minutes

• Resistance training: 25-30 minutes

• Conditioning finisher: 10-15 minutes

A great session to roast body fat would look something like the example below.

The weights used should be sufficiently challenging to leave you in a position of feeling that you could get one more good repetition with excellent technique when you hit the rep range suggested.

Resistance Sets:
A1: Front squat   10-12 reps

A2: Single arm row   12-15 reps on each arm
A3: Jump rope   45 seconds

20-30 seconds rest between exercises and 45-60 seconds rest between each round.

Complete 3 rounds

B1: Heavy kettlebell swing   15-20 reps
B2: Dumbbell press   10-12 reps on each arm
B3: Jump rope   45 seconds

20-30 seconds rest between exercises and 45-60 seconds rest between each round.

Complete 3 rounds

Conditioning Finisher:
A1: 200-400m run
A2: 10-20 burpees
A3: Medicine ball slams

Complete 5 rounds as fast as possible.

Remember, this would be part of a 3-4 session per week plan that is progressed over a number of weeks.

Repeating the same exercises, weights and reps all the time will get you nowhere fast!

4. SLEEP MORE

There's a reason you love sleeping in on Saturday. And it's not just because you don't have to spend 8 hours resisting the urge to punch your boss in the face.

Sleep is so important for developing a lean, athletic-looking body because of the control it exerts over stress and recovery hormones.

Whilst some people can function well as night owls, most of us need the proverbial 8 hours from about 2200-2230 to maintain the correct circadian rhythm which keeps cortisol in check and stimulates the release of growth hormone.

Cortisol is the main stress hormone in the body. It should gradually rise as dawn approaches in order to get you going for the day and then start to fall towards late afternoon – hitting a low during the night when you want to be at your most relaxed.

Unfortunately if you are a 'stress head' who also lacks quality sleep, the whole cycle gets messed up resulting in you not being able to get out of bed to exercise in the morning, and being 'wired' late evening when you should be chilling out.

You won't recover properly leaving you unable to grow lean muscle, crucial for looking great and maintaining a fat-burning metabolism.

Also, as cortisol helps mobilize energy for action, you'll be mobilizing it at the wrong times leading to further fat storage. Get to bed earlier and get up earlier. Just like your Nan said.

5. SUPPLEMENTS FOR HEALTH, RECOVERY, HORMONE BALANCING

I don't recommend many supplements.

I only recommend those that contain ingredients that used to be part of our diet but have largely been lost due to farming, transportation and storage methods, or those which are required to improve recovery and digestion.

Include the following 'supplements' in your fat loss plan.

- Probiotics: Take once per day to get the digestive system working again after years of abuse.
- Fish oil: 4-6g per day is proven to encourage fat loss, help control blood sugar and perform a whole host of positive duties in the brain and immune system.
- Protein: Combined with some carbs, a post-workout protein shake will help you recover better and faster, maintaining lean muscle and a higher metabolic rate.

- Whey protein is the best in terms of bioavailability but it can be argued that vegan sources are a better long-term healthier option. The jury is out, so find what works for you.

- Greens drink: Sink a greens drink as soon as you get up and watch your energy and health improve dramatically. More details below.

6. GO GREEN

You know you should eat more vegetables but if you want the fast results you're demanding, it's going to take more than a couple of lettuce leaves with your sugar-filled baguette.

Ensure you have as much green as possible in every single meal.

Yes, this includes breakfast.

I like spinach or broccoli (pre-steamed the night before) in my omelettes, but a great alternative which I highly recommend even if you eat lots of veg, is a greens drink made from grasses and sometimes powdered vegetables.

This can be blended into fruit smoothies or just mixed with water.

Drunk before you have breakfast, it will help oxygenate your blood, raise your energy levels, build a strong immune system and reduce inflammation – which are all essential for a healthy, energetic, lean body.

So get yourself a 'greens drink' and ensure you eat lots of the following:

- Broccoli
- Cabbage
- Lettuce
- Asparagus
- Kale
- Celery
- Cucumber

7. FAT FLUX

Start all your meals with protein and vegetables as standard.

Then make a decision as to whether you eat fat or carbs with that combination based on whether you have just exercised hard or not.

Carbs and fats both cause a rise in insulin (carbs more so – particularly simple, refined ones).

As insulin is a storage hormone, eating meals high in fat AND carbs at the same time can lead to fat storage.

To avoid this, eat fats in most of your meals and cut out the carbohydrates (other than the natural ones in vegetables).

When you eat carbs in your post-workout meals or on 'high carb' days in the Turbo Transformation, eliminate any fat intake.

This process enables you to get in all the nutrients you want, but at the right times and whilst maintaining fat burning at a high rate.

GO TRANSFORM YOURSELF

If you apply those 'Seven Spells' of Turbo Transformation magic, you will see your body fat and inches drop like a stone. It has been proven time and time again on a wide range of people in countries across the world. The only reason for it not working is if you doubt any of it based on 'what you already know'.

If you are not getting results, what you think you know doesn't work. Sorry.

Try these processes for just seven days and watch the magic begin!

If you are unsure how to piece the fat loss jigsaw together, please visit: www.turbotransformation.com for the daily blueprint including interactive coaching from Jon Le Tocq to take you through every step of the journey.

Don't be another gym statistic!

Find out more about Jon's programs at:

- Storm Force Fitness –
  www.stormforcefitness.com
- Turbo Transformation –
  www.turbotransformation.com
- Guernsey Fitness Camp –
  www.guernseyfitnesscamp.com
- Make friends with Jon on Facebook –
  www.facebook.com/jletocq
- Check out his training videos at –
  www.youtube.com/stormforcefitness

About Jon

Jon is a highly sought-after strength and conditioning coach in his home island of Guernsey, and now across the waters in a variety of countries around the world, having co-authored three global best-selling fitness books.

Never satisfied, he demands a lot of himself and his clients, travelling the world to study and experiment with the best training and nutrition methods on the planet.

Jon is known for training hard himself to test and prove his methods — which he then adapts to match the requirements of members of the public and high-level athletes preparing for battle!

The most common phrase used by Jon's clients is "I wish I had done this years ago" because of the phenomenal results achieved in a surprisingly short time by men and women of all ages.

Don't be another gym statistic!

CHAPTER 2

Releasing The Brakes – Why 'Just Do It' Thinking Won't Get You What You Want

By Dax Moy

How many times have you started a new diet or exercise plan with the best of intentions and resolutions and promising yourself that, 'this time I WILL do this!' only to find that after only a few days (or even hours!) that all of your progress comes to a screeching halt…that your willpower crumbles to dust and that the very things that you promised yourself you wouldn't do are now being done…in supersize?

If you're anything like most people, the answer will be 'HUNDREDS of times' – right?

It's kind of strange when you think about it. On the one hand, we all tell ourselves that losing fat and getting into amazing shape is super-important to our health and happiness; yet whenever we're asked to prove just how important it really is by being committed and diligent in our efforts, we find it almost impossible to go the distance on our promises.

Why is that?

That's a question I used to ask myself all the time when I first set out on my personal training and coaching career. I'd meet people who would often literally burst into tears in my consulting room – because they were so overcome with pain and emotion as they told me "This MUST change!" and "I'm willing to do ANYTHING it takes to get things right this time" and "I simply cannot take living like this any longer!"

It was seriously moving stuff, and I, of course, believed every word of it. Why wouldn't I? After all, THEY believed every word of it too.

They really and truly believed that 'this time, this ONE time, I'm going to damned-well do this,' yet mere days later (or as much as a week or so for the *really* motivated ones) the first cracks would appear in their resolution and willpower.

One missed workout would become two, two would become three and before they knew what was happening, they were back to not working out at all. Same with nutrition and diet as the 'just one won't hurt' mentality asserted itself and was once again proven wrong. One cookie became two, two became a packet and a packet became licence to say, *"Well, now that I've messed up again, what's the point of carrying on?"*

As a trainer and a coach, this left me floating between genuine confusion about what was going on and frustration about never being able to find 'serious clients,' to (I'm ashamed to admit), anger and resentment toward those who I felt were wasting my time and efforts and deliberately trying to make me look bad. (Irrational, I know, yet it often felt that way at the time.)

Then I realised that the fitness and motivational industries had done a real number on both personal trainers and the clients they serve.

Trainers were told that if a client really and truly wants results, they'd do what's asked of them, no questions asked...and that, of course, if they didn't, that they were wasting both their own time and their trainers' because they simply weren't serious enough about getting results. At the same time, those who were trying to lose weight and get into shape were being made to feel that they were lazy, unmotivated and so stupid that they couldn't figure out that an apple was a better choice of snack than a chocolate bar.

In short, getting into great shape was becoming a lose-lose proposition for all concerned. And one that was adversarial in nature too. Trainers were fighting a battle against 'lazy' clients and clients were in combat with diets and exercise programs they hated, and that simply didn't work for them.

The trouble was, despite all this battling, no one was winning... and they couldn't.

So, against the backdrop of all this battling, I realised something that no one else seemed to be talking about. **The way we were approaching fitness and health simply was not working anymore...and perhaps it never did!**

The idea of eating less and moving more sounds so simple and obvious, yet so few people seemed able to pull this off in any way whatsoever, and those that did only managed it for a short period of time at best.

It struck me then that all of the motivational 'just do it... winners never quit and quitters never win... if you can conceive it and believe it you can achieve it' quotes in the world simply weren't working either. 'Just do it' sounded great, but what if 'doing it' is what you're struggling with most of all?

'Winners never quit' sounds cool too, but what if you've never seen yourself as a winner and have never experienced winning in the first place?

'Conceive, believe, achieve' sounds amazing, but what if you really DON'T believe?

No-one was asking these questions, let alone trying to answer them. Instead it seemed that we were simply insisting that accomplishment and achievement was as simple as living the quotes... even though so few seemed to be able to do so.

So I made it *my* business to find the answers. And I realised something pretty quickly...

Most of the failures, struggle, stresses and problems we face in pursuing our goals lie not in the goals themselves (pretty much any goal is achievable when you break it down into logical steps), but rather in the fact that we fail to do the one thing that is guaranteed to help us succeed in our quest to reach them. Trouble is, failing to do that one thing guarantees that we never will!

The one thing?

WE FORGET TO RELEASE THE BRAKES.

Picture this...

You get into your car, start the engine, put your foot on the gas and... nothing. No movement at all, just the noise of the engine turning over.

Confused, you check that the car is in gear, hit the gas a little harder and hear the engine give a satisfying roar as the revs increase – yet once more, nothing. You're going nowhere.

Frustrated now, you floor the gas, the engine screams, the whole car vibrates and starts to roll forward just a little as bit by bit, the power of the engine overcomes the inertia of a ton of glass, metal and upholstery, yet because you're concerned about the noise coming from the engine, the smell of burning rubber coming from the wheels and the intense vibration coming from everywhere you decide to stop....to quit...you'll take your journey another day, you decide.

Just as you're about to switch off the engine and call your mechanic, you look down and experience a Homer Simpson 'Doh!' moment as you realise that you still had your parking brake in place. No wonder you weren't going anywhere!

You release the brake, lightly tap the gas and roll easily and quietly out of the driveway and set out for your destination... at last!

Why the story about cars and brakes?

Because it describes EXACTLY why most of your fitness and fatloss attempts fall flat on their face. In your effort to 'just do it', you're setting out on your journey without doing the most important thing you could possibly do to assure your success.

You're setting out without releasing the brakes!

— Starting a diet while you still have processed, high sugar, high carb food in your cupboards and refrigerator?

Brake!

If you own it you WILL eat it.

— Starting an exercise program without setting aside specific times to exercise?

Brake!

If you can't say EXACTLY when your training will take place, then you're unlikely to train at all. 'Today' or 'later' isn't the same as '6:15 am every day' for example.

— Setting out without a clear purpose and a deep and meaningful reason for pursuing them?

Brake!

A big enough 'why' will keep you on the straight and narrow when times get tough, yet a small one (or none at all) will guarantee you'll quit every time.

These are just 3 examples, yet they clearly show how most attempts at getting into great shape are lost before they even get started, as driving with the brakes on is simply too hard, too tiring, too boring and lack any real power to make anyone want to commit to doing the work required to get the results.

On the other hand, releasing the brakes makes it all very easy for the simple reason that all of your efforts can be used to move you forward – rather than having to fight against the pull of those things that are holding you back.

You 'get' this, right? But how do you actually implement releasing the brakes so that you can benefit from all the forward momentum you're going to gain?

Easy!

Simply identify the biggest 3-5 brakes in each of the following areas:

- **Time** – what time brakes are keeping you from doing what you need to do in order to get the results you want to get? Where is time being used poorly? Where is time being wasted? What could you do to get more time?

- **Inspiration** – what kind of things are present in your life that are sapping your motivation and inspiration? What 'motivation thieves' are currently making life harder for you than it could and should be?

- **Clarity** – what are you not clear about, need to learn more about or want more information about? Lack of clarity is a BIG brake!

- **Relationships** – what relationship brakes are present that are making it hard to focus on your goal? WHO is getting in the way of your progress?

- **Nutrition** – what nutrition brakes are in your way that are keeping you from achieving your goal? Too many carbs? Processed foods? Snacking?

- **Exercise** – What elements of your exercise program are acting like brakes? Exercises you don't like? Gym you hate? Program that takes too long?

Once you've identified at least 3 brakes in each area, identify **WHY** they are brakes and how they actually affect your ability to progress toward your goals.

For instance, a relationship brake may be that you feel guilty about leaving your family for an hour in the evening while you go to the gym, because they already see so little of you due to work commitments. An exercise brake may be that you can't stand cardio training because everyone tells you that you have to do it to get results, and because of this you don't end up training at all.

Identify why each brake IS a brake and how the brake actually stops you: "I feel guilty leaving the house again after getting home from work, so I stay home with the family instead, but end up doing nothing but sitting on the sofa, watching TV, eating…and getting fatter."

It's important that you tell the truth, the whole truth and nothing but the truth while answering these questions. After all, the truth will set you free…as you'll soon see!

Finally, come up with 3-5 solutions that allow you to release each brake in each area where you're stuck.

Feel guilty about coming home late then going back out again?

Could you get up earlier and hit the gym on the way to work? Could you buy some fitness equipment and train at home? Could you make it fun and engage your kids in your plans to get into great shape?

In all 3 examples above, there's a solution for releasing the brakes. Pick one, or better still, create your own.

Do this for all of the primary brakes before you even think of putting your foot 'on the gas' and getting going in pursuit of your goals.

I know what you're thinking. Sounds like a lot of work, right? Maybe, but so is failing. So is starting but never finishing. So is never ever seeing the results you so desperately want to see in return for all your efforts.

Yet the 30 minutes this exercise will take to complete can change your life. Just 30 minutes and the brakes will release and with less effort than ever before you'll be moving along in the direction of your goals.

Just 30 minutes.

Ask the questions. Answer the answers.

Release the brakes and no matter how big your goal, your success is guaranteed…you'll see!

About Dax

Dax Moy is the guy you call when your dreams are too small.

A best-selling author with several titles related to self-development, personal growth, goal-achievement and holistic health as well as being a recognised member of The World Fitness Elite, Dax is a world- renowned expert in human performance – who is regularly sought out for his opinions on developing performance strategies that really work.

Dax has been seen on BBC News, ITV's *'This Morning'* Show, Ch4's 'You Are What You Eat', *CBS News and in The New York Times, The Washington Post, The Financial Times, The Evening Standard* and magazines such as *Men's Health, Men's Fitness, Health and Fitness, Glamour, Vogue* and *Cosmopolitan* among many others.

Dax is known as a coach who's dedicated to bringing out the greatness in others through his laser-focused ability to ask the questions that count, and finding the answers that inspire rapid and dramatic change in his clientele. His clientele includes Royalty, A-list celebrities, Actors, Musicians, Politicians and CEO's.

To learn more about Dax Moy –'The Guy You Call When Your Dreams are Too Small,' and to get a free copy of his special report *'The Biggest Lie - The TRUTH About Why Your Life Isn't Working Out'* visit: www.IAmDaxMoy.com

CHAPTER 3

Be Decisive, Disciplined and Determined

By Nick Berry & Pat Rigsby

Any given evening when you are watching your favorite television program, no doubt you have seen the commercials for weight loss companies that pay celebrities to literally sing their praises and talk about their personal successes with weight loss through using the company's specific program. You can probably name at least a half-dozen weight loss commercials and identify the associated celebrity. Thousands of people respond daily to those advertisements and buy the product or pay to attend the meetings. Why? Because the ad hit them at a "moment" when they realized they need help dropping some pounds and they think, "If that celebrity can do it, that must be the weight loss program I need."

We all have had that "moment" of realization about something in our lives. Something we need to change. How many times do we have that nagging thought in the back of our minds that affects us like (what marketers call) a "drip campaign." You know what I am talking about, when thoughts of doing something about a problem keep "dripping" onto your consciousness telling you, "make a change, make a change, make a change."

There is an old story about a man that came to visit his elderly friend that lived out in the country in a traditional farmhouse. When he

33

arrived the old man was sitting on the front porch in his rocking chair just watching the day go by. Only a few feet from him was his faithful hound dog, Duke. Duke was participating in the same activity as his master, just lying on the porch watching the day go by. During the course of conversation that afternoon, the visiting friend noticed that every few minutes Duke would let out a howl. Curious about this behavior the friend asked the old man, "Why does Duke keep howling like that every few minutes?" The old man replied, "Don't pay any attention to ol' Duke. He's just lying on a rusty nail and it keeps poking him, but it only hurts enough to make him howl, not enough to make him get up."

That story is more true-to-life than most of us want to believe, even when it comes to our health and fitness. It's like we are lying on a rusty nail, but it doesn't hurt enough to do anything about it. We have to ask ourselves, "How did we get to this point?" In regard to health and fitness, how did you get to be twenty or thirty pounds overweight? How did you fall into such bad eating habits? Why do you allow yourself to eat cookies for breakfast rather than oatmeal? Or have that heavily-sugared beverage instead of water. How did you get to that point?

To be sure, there are certain genetic factors that cause us to be wired in certain ways. While I am not a geneticist, I do understand that everyone is wired differently and, as a result, may respond physically and psychologically to various stimuli differently. However, except for very rare situations, most of our bad habits are based on learned behavior. Have you ever spotted obese children in public and noticed, almost exclusively, their parents are also obese? That observation is not made to be demeaning, but to drive home a very important point. Obesity, again, except for rare exceptions, is a learned behavior. Now, some people may be more predisposed to obesity because of certain physiological factors, but for most of us, weight issues are related to learned behavior.

Some people have struggled with their weight their entire lives, while others never had a weight issue until they reached a certain age or until they became more sedentary in their lifestyle. Do you remember the "freshman 15"? This is a phenomenon that occurs when a person enters college for their freshman year. Purportedly there is a tendency to have a noticeable weight gain. The causes of weight gain may be attributable to a fat and carbohydrate-rich cafeteria-style food or fast food on university campuses. Increased alcohol consumption also becomes a factor. Add to this a lack of sleep, stress and decreased levels of exercise, and you have a recipe for weight gain. There have even been university studies completed on this subject. But the point is, changes in diet, lifestyle, mindset, and age can all be factors that get us to a point with our weight and nutritional habits that cause us to scratch our heads and say to ourselves, "How did this happen?"

I (Nick), was very athletic my entire life. As a baseball player in high school and college, I stayed in great shape. The coaches always had me working on muscle development. However, during my college baseball career as a catcher, I was not able to continue in that position because of extensive pain in my knees. I was moved to first base for the remainder of my college years. I went on from college to become a fitness trainer, and then moved into fitness facility ownership and then consulting. While I was a trainer, I kept myself physically fit. However, when I moved behind a desk and was removed from the daily exposure to the fitness equipment, I found I was working out less and less as the months and years went by. I also became less disciplined in my eating habits. Within five years, I had gradually gained forty pounds of excess weight, my muscle mass had deteriorated, and my nutritional habits were less than desirable.

The breaking point for me came after getting the results from an insurance physical. The results were not terrible, but there were a couple of things that were marginal. Being a lifetime athlete and a fitness trainer, my reaction was actually that of anger. I was angry that I let myself get to the point where there were some health issues, even if they were only marginal. That set me on a course for change. I was going to focus on better nutrition and get back to a regular workout routine. The nutritional part for me was easy. I set my mind to make the change and never looked back. However, the injuries causing me to have to relinquish my catching position in college were still plaguing me. So, I found someone who was able to determine the problem and discovered the issue stemmed back to the ineffective way I was trained when I began strength training at the age of fourteen. I received very little training on movement and mobility – which resulted in injury with long-term residual effect. Every time I would work out it would be very painful which discouraged me from sticking to a fitness routine. Now, after proper rehabilitation and training, the pain I experienced for years is resolved.

Today I continue to eat properly and train regularly. The result has been continuous weight loss, with no plateau, over the course of six months. To date, I have lost thirty-five pounds and have five more to go. I feel I have more mobility now than when I was a college athlete. From my personal experience, I know it is very important to get a nutrition and workout plan and follow it. By a nutritional plan, I don't mean a complicated diet. I mean following the basic principles of having a protein and vegetable at every meal. I found people who knew what worked and I did what they told me. There was no magic to it. It was simple and basic. I just had to follow it.

What will your breaking point be? For me it was getting angry at the results of an insurance physical. There has to be a breaking point. You may be lying on the proverbial rusty nail like the story of Duke earlier in this chapter, and that nail just hurts enough for you to howl and complain about it. But, it doesn't hurt enough for you to get up and do something about it. What will it take for you? How many times has your doctor told you that you need to lose weight? How many times will you look in the mirror and say to yourself, "I really need to do something about that." How long will you allow yourself to become exhausted by walking up a flight of stairs? Everyone needs to experience a breaking point. I encourage you to make a decision to take care of yourself nutritionally and physically before you experience a physiological consequence that has irreversible results. It is no secret that poor nutrition and poor physical health can lead to a multitude of diseases. Don't wait until disease has set in before making a change.

For anyone that wants to lose weight, there is a simple phrase you must commit to memory, "You cannot out-train nutrition." Many people think that if they work out enough they can eat whatever they want to eat and still get the same results. However, there is more to the story. Proper nutritional practices are essential to good health and fitness. Diets don't have to be complicated. The purpose of this chapter is not to give you specific details about what to eat, but to encourage you to have the discipline to find a nutritional program that will benefit you. If you have to transition to eating differently, start by eating smaller portions at mealtime. Then gradually take away foods that are not benefiting you and replace them with more nutritional foods. You have to make it a lifestyle change.

Effective weight loss requires proper nutritional habits as well as a physical work out on a regular basis. While walking is definitely considered exercise, you need to eventually get to a workout routine that will make you sweat. Of course, consult your physician before beginning any type of exercise program. For most people, there will not be any reason you shouldn't work out. In fact, the medical community is constantly encouraging exercise. However, there will be the rare occasion that a doctor may limit your routine based on your current physical condition.

You really don't need expensive equipment to get a proper workout. Using just your body weight, there are very effective exercise routines that can make a significant impact. While each person's results will vary, with very few exceptions, you should experience consistent improvement in your fitness level if you are eating properly and exercising properly. If you plateau during the weight loss process, it is an indication that you need to make modifications to your nutrition or workout plan.

It is always helpful to seek out professional help for your diet and work out program. However, it is not absolutely necessary. For those that are reading this and have already formulated an excuse in your mind that you can't do this because you can't afford to pay a nutritionist and a personal trainer, let me squash that thought right now. This does not have to be a financially draining proposition. Especially with Internet access, you will have no trouble finding the help and advice you need to make the necessary changes to put you on the road to a healthier lifestyle.

Results are a key component to maintaining your routine. If you change your diet and don't see any progress in weight loss, it can become very discouraging. On the other hand, seeing results can be very motivating. **Results** are one of those key factors that drive you to become more successful in whatever you do. Experiencing results in weight loss is no different. Allow your success to be a motivating factor. Set specific goals for yourself, but make sure they are reasonable and attainable. Don't be afraid to set some "stretch" goals. Those are goals that you will have to really "stretch" yourself mentally and physically to achieve. The word "mentally" is used very intentionally in that last sentence because there is a psychology to weight loss and fitness that you must realize. You have to determine mentally what you will achieve before you will see any accomplishment. What is your overall objective? Is it just weight loss or do you also want to achieve a more sculpted body? How much weight do you want to lose? How will you know when you have achieved your goal? What will you do about maintaining your weight loss and not putting those pounds back on? The answers to all of these questions and more have to be formulated in your mind so that you can become as specific as possible in your goal setting.

Another very important psychological component to your success is **discipline**. In fact, without discipline you will not succeed. Discipline will be the driving factor for perseverance and consistency in your nutritional habits as well as your workout routine. There will be times you will not want to work out, but you will have to make yourself do it. There will be times you want to pull into that fast food restaurant and taste those french fries and sugar-laden soft drink, but discipline will push you to drive past. Some people allow themselves to have "cheat" days or "reward" days. I found that I didn't need to do that because I mentally conditioned myself to know that will not contribute to my long-term goal. My experience has been that after three or four months my routine became habitual. Since I travel a great deal, you would think that would become a problem for my weight loss plan. But, it doesn't matter where I go, I can find a way to eat in a disciplined fashion and continue my workouts even being on the road.

I encourage people to mix up their routine as much as possible. Try to eat as wide a variety of foods as possible so it does not become mundane. There are a plethora of resources on the Internet to help you find the right foods to eat that will be nutritionally sound for you. Your workout routine also needs to have variety. While you need to focus on strength and endurance training, you don't have to do the same exercise routine over and over to accomplish that goal. Again, there are plenty of free resources on the Internet to keep your routine ever changing so it doesn't become monotonous. My intention here is not to give you specific diets or routines, but rather to encourage you to adopt the right mindset and discipline.

In summary, let's review what we have discussed.

- First, you need to make a firm decision to eat healthy and exercise effectively on a regular basis.

- Second, set reasonable and achievable goals as well as some stretch goals.

- Third, establish your nutritional plan based on your research and include as many healthy foods as possible.

- Fourth, establish your workout routine based on your research and keep variety in your plan so you don't get bored.

- Fifth, be disciplined and consistent in your eating habits and your workout.

- Sixth, if you plateau, re-evaluate to determine what you are doing wrong and make the necessary changes.

Finally, don't ever give up! Make a commitment to a lifetime lifestyle change!

About Pat

Pat Rigsby is an author, consultant and fitness entrepreneur as well as the Co-Owner of over a dozen businesses within the fitness industry. The Fitness Consulting Group, owned by Nick Berry and himself, is the leading business development organization in the fitness industry. The Fitness Consulting Group provides resources, coaching programs and consulting to give you everything you need to start or grow your personal training or fitness-related business.

In addition to his business coaching and consulting work, Pat is also the Co-Owner of two of the fastest- growing franchises in the fitness industry, Fitness Revolution and Athletic Revolution.

Fitness Revolution is the leading training-based franchise in the world and designed specifically to allow quality fitness professionals to develop successful businesses. You can learn more at: www.fitnessrevolutionfranchise.com.

Athletic Revolution is the top youth fitness and sports performance franchise in the world today and the leading resource for long-term athletic development for kids ages 6-18. You can learn more about Athletic Revolution at: www.myathleticrevolution.com.

For additional information, you can read Pat's popular newsletter serving over 65,000 fitness professionals worldwide or learn more about all of his offerings at: www.fitbusinessinsider.com.

About Nick

Nick Berry has spent his entire career as an Entrepreneur in the fitness industry. His experience has given him the opportunity to become a Business Coach and Consultant, and co-owner of dozens of other businesses, which have allowed him to help thousands of other small business owners, both in and out of the fitness industry.

Nick co-founded, co-owns, and continues to build the Athletic Revolution™ and Fitness Revolution™ franchise systems. Athletic Revolution™ (www.myathleticrevolution.com) is a youth-based sports performance franchise which began in 2009 and currently has over 30 franchise units. Fitness Revolution™ (www.fitnessrevolutionfranchise.com) is an adult fitness franchise, which began in January 2011, and currently has over 50 franchise units.

Nick partnered with Pat Rigsby in 2005 and they continue to operate Fitness Consulting Group, (www.fitbusinessinsider.com) from which they offer their fitness business consulting programs. He has helped build and co-owns the International Youth Conditioning Association, which is considered the premier international authority on youth conditioning and athletic development (www.iyca.org). He also was a co-author of the International Best Selling *Total Body Breakthroughs* book in the spring of 2011.

CHAPTER 4

Hierarchy To Successful Fat Loss

By Matt Hancocks

I have always been interested in fitness and fat loss and have degrees in sport and exercise science and sports therapy, worked with thousands of clients on and offline, and my biggest frustration was when my weight loss clients hadn't lost the expected amount of weight during assessment. I knew I was giving them some quality training and nutrition protocols, and they swore blindly that they were following it to the letter, so why did they not get the expected results?

For the most part it's mindset, you cannot get the results with your body until you have your mind set on the task at hand. Fat loss is about making the correct choices. Everything in your life is a reflection of a choice you have made. If you want a different result, you have to make a different choice. It's as simple and complex as that. It may seem a little black and white, but I truly believe we make things harder on ourselves by continually making excuses: "Not enough time"; "I like a drink at the weekend"; and my favourite, "Life is too short."

I'm not saying it's easy. There are certain practicalities you have to overcome, but at the end of the day if it's important to you, you'll find a way – if not, you'll find an excuse.

The ideas and attitudes with which a person approaches a situation, *especially* when these are seen as being difficult to alter, refer to a

43

person's mindset. I often found that I wanted results more than my clients. Sometimes this still happens, but this is often because I know how they will feel when they achieve their goals. Fat Loss Clients think instead about the bad habits they have to overcome, which often seem overwhelming. At the end of the day nobody can want it for you, you have to want it for yourself. The mind is the master and controller of everything. Our thoughts, in my humble opinion, hold the key to our future; therefore, negative thoughts only serve to hold us back.

Whatever you hold in your mind on a consistent basis is exactly what you will experience in your life – Anthony Robbins

To achieve anything worthwhile in life – you must take positive action to implement change. Set a goal and be mindful that from that day forward everything you do will either take you a step closer or further away from that goal. Fat loss is no exception, so here are a few suggestions to help you implement a change:

- Visualise yourself and your goals, with a set timeframe.

- Refill your cupboards with healthy food.

- Train with others and make yourself accountable by telling others what you are doing and why.

- Enjoy what you do; training should never be a chore.

- Think one positive thought every morning, as this will change your whole day.

- Change the way you train, from this day forward.

One of the main reasons why people don't get results in health clubs or don't achieve their fat loss goals is due to faulty programming. Achieving a successful **mindset** comes before anything else, but then other elements must draw our focus. Most people currently ignore the key principles of harmonizing hormones through nutrition, not realizing this is the foundation to achieving results. Nutrition is key to gaining successful fat loss as you cannot out-train a poor diet, but that's another chapter all together. I'm going to focus on the movement that matters, as when it comes to training, there are some key systems to focus on for effective fat loss.

Born out of years of personal research, studying with the world's leading functional medicine doctors, professional athlete conditioners, and other therapists and professionals across many disciplines, I have developed this simple model to encapsulate what you need to implement in order to achieve optimum fat loss.

Diagram: Hierarchy for Successful Fat Loss

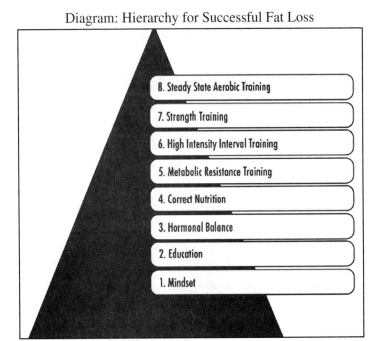

8. Steady State Aerobic Training

7. Strength Training

6. High Intensity Interval Training

5. Metabolic Resistance Training

4. Correct Nutrition

3. Hormonal Balance

2. Education

1. Mindset

The first goal of training for fat loss is to elevate your metabolism, or more correctly your resting metabolic rate (RMR) by increasing muscle mass –because this means you will burn more calories (energy) every day. Your RMR is based on the energetic costs of keeping the cells in our bodies alive. Therefore your basal metabolic rate stays the same no matter what you do, and therefore makes up the bulk of energy you burn. Burning extra calories (energy) in addition to the RMR when working out is great, but the impact on total energy burned is fairly small compared to the total RMR. Muscle is the only tissue that uses fat for energy. Your metabolism is almost exclusively tied to your Lean Body Mass, therefore the more lean mass you have, the higher your metabolism, and vice versa. So in order to achieve a metabolically- charged body, we need to engage in correct strength training programs.

The second thing you need to be applying is the integration of activities that burn calories (energy) and elevate EPOC. (Exercise post oxygen consumption) which is informally referred to as metabolic afterburn. Which, by Wikipedia definition, is:

A measurably increased rate of oxygen intake following strenuous activity intended to erase the body's "oxygen debt."

This involves activities with work/rest formula that involves getting you to work 85-100% of your maximum heart rate. Working at this intensity for short bursts will use a different source of fuel rather than oxygen, and is referred to as anaerobic training and will raise both your EPOC and RMR significantly.

So therefore, your workout time needs to include both strength train-ing and anaerobic conditioning because both contribute to muscle building and they burn energy. The magic of strength and anaerobic training is that they boost your overall metabolic rate, burn a lot of energy in a short period of time, and elevate the RMR by increasing the amount of lean mass you have.

This type of training is best experienced through metabolic resistance training (MRT) and involves the use of a load, which you move with intensity.

Although moderate intensity aerobic training is universally regarded as being heart protective and the ideal vehicle for fat burning, there is compelling evidence that shows that anaerobic exercise is evenly matched with regards to heart health. Interestingly, recent studies have shown that anaerobic exercise is a vastly superior protocol for fat burning than it's less intense aerobic counterpart. Contrary to popular belief, kettlebells, medicine balls, power bags and the like, performed at high exertion levels can surpass bike riding and running at conferring increased aerobic capacity! Moreover, strength training and anaerobic conditioning used this way will burn fat whilst building lean tissue, affecting the body differently than aerobic training – which tends to break down lean tissue regardless of the intensity of that aerobic exercise.

Ultimately metabolic conditioning can be summed up in two points:

1. Metabolic training can match endurance training for aerobic benefit.

2. Metabolic training with varying and mixed exercise modalities avoids specificity of adaptation, increasing functional strength.

This revolutionary combination of resistance training intervals and high intensity cardiovascular exercise, ensures that your metabolism is sufficiently shocked for 24-48 hours after the workout, further increasing your body's metabolism. If you only have time to train 2-3 times per week, MRT will give you the best 'bang for your buck.'

High Intensity anaerobic Interval Training:
(Include this, if you train 3-4 times per week.)
This type of training, informally recognised as HIIT training, can be completed independently of MRT work and is completed at high intensity, so that you use energy already stored in your muscles, since the oxygen doesn't have time to come through the lungs, transfer to the red blood cells and be transported to the working muscles. As a by product of using this stored fuel, the body produces a waste product known as lactic acid. This is the unpleasant heaviness feeling you have when training at this high intensity, the upside for weight loss is that your metabolism stays elevated for several hours as your body will have to deal with the lactic acid build up and try to return the body back to it's neutral state. This process takes several hours, thus increasing your metabolism and calorie burn – 'way after' the session has ended.

An example would be to do 10 second sprints with 20 seconds recovery, repeated up to 20 times.

High Intensity aerobic Interval Training:
(Include this, if you train 4-5 times per week.)

This follows the same principles as above except you are staying at 70 – 80% of your predicted maximum. You could repeat 400m runs for example, with the rest period being the same as the time it took to complete the 400m. The intensity would be less than anaerobic intervals, so if sprinting is 100% you would be running at around 70-80%. This would work with rowers, bikes, stair climbs or hill walking. Anything really.

Strength Training:
(Include this, if you train 4-5 times per week.)

This type of training involves working with weights to cause an overload and can be completed in many different ways, but we have included what we consider to be two of the best.

Density training

This involves doing a number of exercises where you lift reasonably heavy load for a certain amount of time. When you have completed that set number of exercises, you then repeat each exercise for the same amount of time but with a greater resistance (10-20%). The object being to match the repetitions of the exercise in the same given time frame.

For example:

	Round 1 - 40/20	Round 2 - 40/20
A1 – Lat pull down	40 kg	48 kg
A2 – Squat to push press	6kg	8kg
A3 – Chest press	12kg	14kg

Dynamic training

Another option is Dynamic training where you complete a certain number of repetitions in 2 circuits of say 3-4 exercises.

For example:

A1 – Press ups (40 reps)
A2 – Squats (30 reps)
A3 – Stationary lunge to push press (25 reps each side)

Perform A1 for as many reps as possible with good form, then proceed to A2. Perform A2 to failure, then proceed to A3. Perform A3 to failure.

Return to A1 and repeat this until you have completed the prescribed number of reps for each exercise. The number of sets will vary each workout. After all reps are completed, rest for 30 seconds and proceed to your dynamic interrupt (2 exercises that are designed to be more metabolic). 20 inch worms and 40 Squat jumps, for example. Rest for 90 seconds before moving on to B1-B3. Follow the same principles as the first circuit, rest for 30 seconds and then finish off with 2-3 metabolic exercises which I like to call the dynamic finisher.

This is a fantastic way to strength train as no specific rest time between the strength exercises is given, so you simply work to your capabilities and monitor progress. You would not do a HIIT training session after completion of this exercise routine, but do it at a different time on the same day, for maximum benefit.

Steady-state High Intensity aerobic Training:
(Include this, if you train 5-6 times per week.)
This involves continuous movement such as a spin class, running or rowing for example but done at high intensity. But not so high that you begin to work without oxygen, but keeping within what is called your lactate threshold. For most people this is 70-80% of max heart rate. You will not work hard enough to increase EPOC significantly or RMR post exercise.

Steady-state Moderate Intensity aerobic Training:
(Include this, if you train more than 6 times per week.)
This again is any continuous movement, but at a lower intensity of about 60-70% of your max heart rate. It refers to activity really, like a walk in the park for example. It won't burn a lot of calories and will not increase muscle or EPOC and should therefore be completed time permitting.

PUTTING IT ALL TOGETHER

These recommendations are perhaps the opposite from what you typically read in mainstream media that will advise long-duration cardiovascular work, progressing to Interval Training and then strength training to sculpt, once you are in shape!

The approach I have laid out here will attack your fat-loss goals from the opposite direction, and you will get more 'bang-for-your-buck.' In today's hectic lifestyle, the number one excuse for lack of exercise is lack of time. We all have 24 hours in the day, its what we prioritize with that time that makes the difference.

Using this hierarchy, you will be able to better manage your exercise time so you workout smarter rather than longer – choosing the best programming for the time you have available.

About Matt

Matt Hancocks is a thought leader, speaker and facilitator of studio systems development. With background degrees in Sport & Exercise Science, Sports Therapy and owner of **elev8 fitness studio** in the U.K, he has over 15 years of experience working with clients – helping them achieve breakthrough goals in health, wellbeing, weight loss and performance. As a rehabilitation specialist and sports conditioner, Matt has worked with some of Yorkshires elite sports men and women.

Matt understands what it takes to run a successful studio that integrates multi- disciplines, utilizes systems that generate results and create a strong referral system. His knowledge, understanding and passion has helped him become a leading coach in the industry, a credible speaker, mentor and is the studio systems master trainer for PT-professionals.

Facilitating groups, corporations and individuals, as a European speaker, performance coach and mentor, Matt has helped a number of studio start up's and consults to many Personal Trainers in the field of weight loss training systems and studio success strategies.

Matt truly understands the multi-disciplined approach that is needed for fitness and wellbeing studios of the future, and has developed turnkey systems for PT professionals and studios to follow and be successful.

CHAPTER 5

Educating The Entrepreneur

By Shawn Guiney

You are an entrepreneur, middle-aged, married with three kids and a dog. You have a successful business and are living the good life. You go for your yearly checkup and BAM, the bad news. The doctor informs you that you have pre-diabetes, high blood pressure, and need to lose 25-40 pounds as soon as possible. After a long talk with your doctor and a prescription for a statin to help control your blood pressure, you try to decide what to do. You take a long, hard look in the mirror and start wondering what happened to the person you were twenty years ago; you enjoyed walking the dog, playing with the kids, coaching baseball, and even going out for 'happy hour'. How did things get so out of control? Now, you are 50 pounds overweight, graying and middle-aged. The lines on your face show the stressful, sleepless nights of running a successful business that takes up all of your time.

You worry about how you will find time to get into shape when you have a business to run. As the owner you have endless responsibilities: overseeing finance, marketing, sales, ad designs, web design and content in addition to the work that you are solely accountable for completing. After climbing the mountain of adversity that an entrepreneur faces, this should be the point in your life where you get a pat on the back for being one of the 27 million small businesses that attribute to 60-80% of the jobs in the United States. This should be a proud moment seeing how 69% of new businesses last 2 years, only 44% last 4 years, and you beat the 49% of businesses that don't make it to 5 years. Most importantly, you have stayed in business well past the 7 year mark—something that only 31% of businesses accomplish. Now the doctor tells you that your health is in jeopardy; it just doesn't seem fair. How can you possibly find time to exercise and take care of your health? Suddenly, the truth of reality sets in. In the midst of this you hear the voice of reason, "After accomplishing everything that you have with your career, getting back into shape will be easy." So you do what anyone else would do, get in your car and head to the local fitness center.

With a desire to make changes in your life, the first week at the gym is smooth sailing. After five solid days at the gym, your total weight loss is 1.5 pounds. Now you are really getting into the routine, you add more weight to the machines used in the circuit area and increase your speed on the treadmill. However, things came up at work and you were only able to make it to the gym 3 times. With the work schedule becoming more hectic, you find yourself sacrificing your time at the gym in order to tie together loose ends at the office. By week 5 you were only able to make it to the gym 1 day. Weight loss did not occur; in fact you gained an additional 4 pounds! This was a result of the business taking up more time than usual and you going back to old eating habits. By now, your routine is totally out of rhythm. The same dilemma plays back over and over in your mind, "How can I possibly take care of my business and my health at the same time? If I take time away I lose money, and if I don't I lose my health." As a result, you maintain your unused gym membership and begin to search the internet for advice on how to do things at home or at work. Eventually, giving up is the only option and it is easy to convince yourself that your poor health is a genetic problem that cannot be solved without losing something else in return.

This is just one typical example of an entrepreneur who is having a hard time getting in shape, while still being a dedicated business professional. The truth is, there are many solutions; although, not one of them are some sort of magic pill or the next piece of equipment that is going to achieve your goals for you. There is, however, a recipe for success—diligence and hard work. The key concept is to be smart about your approach while avoiding the urge to over-analyze information and hopping program to program for the next quick fix. This will allow you to stop thinking and begin acting. In order to get your health back, it is vital that you lay down a foundation for your success.

For the entrepreneur in particular a gym membership is not the option because you are running a business, there are too many people at the gym, and you are otherwise distracted from your goals. It is vitally important to find an alternate means to reach your goals by first knowing what form of exercise is right for you. Look at this check list and see what you can manage and start there!

- Choose an activity you enjoy; you are more likely to stick with it. Do not do something because you think it's a popular activity. If having people exercise with you is important then join a class, club, or form your own group. When working out with a partner, be sure to choose someone with a similar fitness level to avoid working too hard or not hard enough at the beginning stages.

- When starting out, ease into a program and start making it a way of life for yourself. Remember, you should not be trying to make up for all the years you have not exercised in the first few workouts. Because your body is unaccustomed to exercise, realize that you may be stiff or sore after the first day. This soreness is due to lactic acid buildup and will pass as you continue to work the muscles. If you overdo it the first day, you could be turned off from exercising.

- Engage in more than one activity. Anything can become boring or monotonous. If you like cycling and swimming then alternate these activities. Remember to choose activities that can still be done during bad weather. You want to exercise year round, not just in the spring or summer. A good program incorporates aerobic, strength, and flexibility components; aim for all-around conditioning.

- When choosing your activity be sure to consider the availability of facilities around you and the personal cost that accompanies it. Some people feel they will attend more regularly if they join a club or hire a personal trainer. Others choose to buy or make equipment and workout at home.

- When possible, exercise at the same time each day and treat it as an appointment on your planner. Consistency is the key to results-driven exercise; once you have a routine it becomes natural.

- If you are male over 35 or female over 40, or have any pre-existing health concerns, please see your doctor to receive medical clearance to participate in exercise. There may be a valid reason why you should limit your participation or not exercise at all.

Once you have completed the checklist and thought about the things you can do to create a fitness lifestyle for yourself come to terms with three things:

1. why you are beginning the program;

2. what the benefits are; and

3. how they directly relate to your health and success.

While you give those questions some thought, let me inform you why exercise might very well make you more money.

General exercise has been proven to help:

- Manage stress

- Improve Concentration

- Improve moods

- Clear your mind and help you unwind

- Improve self-confidence

- Meet new friends/business partners

- Build healthy lungs and blood vessels

• Build endurance, core strength, and flexibility

If even the first three benefits in that list don't spark your enthusiasm to get healthy then see it as a win/win. If you workout and take care of your health you can make more efficient and effective decisions for your business, resulting in more money, time, and freedom for you and your family. Most importantly, you will be able to recover your health, get the monkey off your back that the doctor keeps telling you about and ensure endless opportunities for your future.

Here are four exercise protocols that will help change your life: Circuit Training, High Intensity Interval Training, Tabata, and Metabolic Resistance Training. All four are good; the best results come to those that are most determined. It is like Ralph Waldo Emerson said, "As to methods, there may be a million and then some, but principles are few. The man who grasps principles can successfully select his own methods." These protocols are proven scientific principles to live by, that you can fall back on over and over again for the rest of your life without fail. It is like being a entrepreneur, once you know how to do business for yourself there is no other way.

I. CIRCUIT TRAINING (CT)

This is a form of conditioning that combines resistance training and high-intensity aerobics. It is designed to target muscular strength as well as muscular endurance. An exercise "circuit" is one completion of all prescribed exercises in the program. When one circuit is complete, you begin the first exercise again for another circuit. Traditionally, the time between exercises in CT is short, often with rapid movement to the next exercise. Most circuits commercial gyms have set up consist of 8-12 machines that target specific body parts. I find that you really only need at least 5 which are chest press, leg press, lat pull (row or pull down), should press, and a good core stability exercise.

II. HIGH-INTENSITY INTERVAL TRAINING (HIIT)

Also known as sprint interval training, HIIT is an enhanced form of interval trainingthat focuses on cardiovascular exercise. It is a strategy that alternates periods of short intense aerobic exercise with recovery periods. These short, intense workouts provide improved athletic capacity and conditioning, improved glucose metabolism, and improved fat burning. A HIIT session consists of a warm up period of exercise, followed by six to ten repetitions of high intensity exercise, separated by medium intensity exercise, and ending with a period of cool down exercise. The high intensity exercise should be done at near maximum. The medium exercise should be about 50% intensity. The number of repetitions and length of each depends on the exercise. The goal is to do at least six cycles, and have the entire HIIT session between fifteen and twenty minutes. HIIT is an excellent way to maximize a workout in limited time. I find this protocol to work best with the elliptical machine because I work as hard with my arms as I do my legs, try it and see what you think.

III. TABATA METHOD

A popular regimen based on a 1996 study uses 20 seconds of ultra-intense exercise followed by 10 seconds of rest, repeated continuously for 4 minutes (8 cycles). It is great to use with cardio equipment and body weight calisthenics. Try this protocol with a rower, pushups or squats and tell me you can't see how effective it is.

IV. METABOLIC RESISTANCE TRAINING (MRT)

A protocol that utilizes large muscle groups with compound exercises. There is little rest in between exercises in an effort to maximize calorie burn and increase metabolic rate during and after the workout. MRT is high intensity exercise with Crossfit being the extreme. Intense exercises are repeated in a circuit with little to no rest in order to push the body to its absolute limit. This training is usually reserved for seasoned athletes and the military so make sure this is what you build up to over time.

Incorporating each of these 4 protocols into your workouts begins the transition into your new fitness lifestyle. While your goal is to improve in all the fitness components which are cardiovascular endurance, muscular strength and endurance, flexibility, and body composition (muscle to fat ratio), the two things that are analyzed for measurable improvements are VO2 Max and EPOC.

VO2 max is your body's ability to use oxygen during cardiovascular exercise and lasts roughly 24 hours while EPOC measures how well your body recovers 48-72 hours later.

Every successful entrepreneur sets goals and has a plan. Here is a way that has worked to help many reach their exercise goals: You will want to target the whole body to get a synergistic flow of intensity to guarantee the most calories burned. You should first start with CT using body weight calisthenics and HIIT for cardio. Comfort level will determine your pace as you perform as many sets and reps in a specific amount of time as you feel possible. Don't fall into the habit of starting a workout and waiting until you are fully recovered before performing the next set. How many times can you perform each of the five following exercises (for 8-12 reps per exercise) in 5 minutes?

(Pushing movement) Pushups   8-12 reps

(Legs) Squats   8-12 reps

(Pulling movement) Inverted Rows   8-12 reps

(Core) Stability ball rollouts   8-12 reps

(HIIT cardio) Sprint 30 seconds - Light jog/Brisk walk 15 seconds

There you have it, the fitness protocols that will allow you to get into shape at home, in the office, or at the gym. This efficient and effective strategy will cut down your workout time by two-thirds. Make sure to always work towards progressing in your routine or activity, just like you would in business. This will allow you to avoid plateaus.

About Shawn

Shawn Guiney, aka the Fitness Physician, BA, IYCA Youth Fitness Specialist, Certified Nutrition Specialist, Certified Personal Trainer, Crossfit Level 1 is a passionate, caring individual with 10 years of experience working with entrepreneurs and working professionals.

Shawn is the owner of Exercise Explorers Academy, CT. He prides himself on truly understanding the unique challenges associated with being an entrepreneur and owning a business or working long days as a professional and trying to take care of his health.

His expertise is in mastering new workout techniques and illustrating those techniques to his clients in a unique way that they can comprehend and implement in their life. He teaches lifestyle fitness that is efficient and effective for the busy Mom, Dad, Entrepreneur and Professional that is short on time, ensuring fast results. Shawn is sought after by small business owners, doctors and nurses throughout Southeastern CT and Long Island, NY. He works with clients at his facility, in home personal training, through email, Skype video messaging and feels that the more he makes himself available to his clients, the more results they will see.

His motto is: *"To Enhance the lives of those he touches through fitness and nutritional advice."*

Shawn's first responsibility is to the improvement of his clients and readers. He has worked with over 500 clients in a **very** short period of time and considers everyone who uses his facility to be a part of his fitness family.

For more information talked about in this chapter, workouts following the protocols, nutrition information and a community that will support your endeavors, please check out: www.eeatoday.com/fadfreefitness

CHAPTER 6

Lose Weight By Losing Your Mind

By Priscilla Freed

What would you say is the hardest part about losing weight? Is it the diet? The exercise? The disciplined lifestyle you must develop? You may agree that it's a combination of all these factors. Most of us have participated in some kind of temporary fitness or diet plan at one point in our lives – and probably don't want to admit to the ones that were fad diets. We've given up our favorite foods, drunk shake concoctions, exercised relentlessly. We may have even gotten sucked into the latest get-skinny-quick scheme because we heard it helped a Hollywood star "drop 10 pounds in 10 days." Yet, we usually end up disappointed when we gain the pounds lost (and then some) after we stop the program. Why is this? Could there be a deeper underlying issue responsible for failure at our weight loss endeavors than the diet program itself? The answer is a resounding YES. The reason you don't succeed is because of your mindset.

WHAT ARE YOU THINKING?

Having a healthy mindset is so important that I propose it to be the single determining factor responsible for your *long-term* weight-loss success. The problem is that we often underestimate how our thinking affects our behaviors, which can make or break our goals.

My experience with an eighth grade classmate years ago clearly demonstrates how your mind should be the first part of your body you strive to change in order to experience victory in your weight-loss efforts. When I was in middle school, one of my classmates had a roller-skating birthday party. Her mother crammed me and her other friends into her van, and off we went to a roller-rink. On the drive there, Sally kept saying, "I'm gonna fall and break my wrist. I'm scared. I'm gonna fall and break my wrist." Even as we walked from the van to the rink's entrance, I'll never forget how I wanted to slap her because she kept repeating her fears about breaking her wrist. Can you guess what happened that afternoon? Even at 13 years old, my instincts told me that Sally's thinking would result in a self-fulfilling prophecy. In fact, we only spun around the rink a few times when…CRASH! What do you think she did? Sally fell and broke her wrist! I still have the picture of us in our caps and gowns at eighth grade graduation to remind me about the power of our thoughts. There's Sally next to me – in a cast.

Sally's forecasted fate was my first experience with the fact that, "as a man thinketh, so is he." At the time, I didn't realize the profundity of this truth: *You are what you believe you are.* While it may not be true in actuality (i.e., you believe you're fat despite being a size two), your thoughts are so powerful that your beliefs truly become your reality. And, both consciously and subconsciously, you will behave in such a way as to ensure that *your* reality matches up with your beliefs. Whatever belief you have of yourself (what I call the *internal you*) will be manifested in your outward appearance (the *external you*). How does this relate to following a fad-free fitness regimen?

TO ACHIEVE LONG-TERM RESULTS, YOU MUST CHANGE YOUR MINDSET

You can follow just about any diet or fitness fad and see results. Yes, I did just say that. Pick any popular weight-loss or exercise program, follow it religiously, and I guarantee you will lose weight and trim up your figure. You could do something extreme such as fast for ten days and you'll lose weight. Or do what most people do: Work out with a personal trainer, join a boot camp, and even go to the gym to walk the treadmill. I guarantee you'll see some measure of improvement in your overall fitness. In fact, it's actually easy to lose weight and firm your muscles. What's difficult is maintaining your results long-term.

So, how do you do this? Just as you need a plan to succeed at your weight loss goals, it is absolutely essential to have a plan for changing your mindset. Would you set a goal to lose 50 pounds but continue the same habits that led you to gain them in the first place?...Of course not. You will need an exercise program, a meal plan, a daily schedule, an accountability group, a trainer, etc. You're going to have to be disciplined about following a daily regimen if you're going to accomplish your goal. The problem with these types of plans is that you're usually addressing the symptoms of the changes you want to make in your body, not the causes.

Whatever program you're following is usually geared towards fixing the *external you* without truly addressing the issues that plague the *internal you*. Yet, it's the *internal you* that's caused what you're trying to change in the *external you*! Usually, training your thinking is not at the forefront of this plan. It sometimes comes as a by-product – if you're successful at reaching your goal. But even if you're successful, old habits often have their way of sneaking back into your lifestyle because their underlying cause wasn't addressed.

Healthy thinking is absolutely essential to having a fad-free lifestyle in which you enjoy life-long success. So, why don't most people and most programs deal with changing your thinking – the internal you? Because it's hard! You have to be willing to do the work. And how many of us want to lose weight slowly? Very few. Just as we often want quick solutions when it comes to weight loss, we're not willing to do the work of changing our mindset because it's a process that takes time. And while you'll enjoy a measure of success on most fitness programs, if you haven't changed the patterns that originally led you to your weight gain, most weight lost will come back with a vengeance after you stop the program. Therefore, unless you change your internal wiring, much of what you worked so hard to accomplish eventually disappears. You can change the outside temporarily, but it won't stay changed until you permanently change the inside.

How can you change the internal you so that you enjoy long-term results? It's actually a simple three-step formula. The change doesn't have to be difficult – but you must be willing to make the effort. You will be rewarded with life-long success if you following this process.

THREE STEPS TO MASTERING A HEALTHY MINDSET

1. Identify your negative feelings, beliefs, and behaviors.

Your mindset is affected by three interrelated areas: Your feelings, beliefs, and behaviors. Your feelings affect your beliefs, which affect your behaviors, which affect your feelings, and so on. This cycle can lead to success or failure at your weight-loss goals depending on whether it's fueled by positive or negative feelings. Therefore, the first thing you must do to create a healthy mindset is to identify negative *feelings* you have about yourself. Here are some questions to help you get started: Do you feel depressed when you look at yourself in pictures? Are you unhappy with how your body looks? Are you obsessed with certain body parts you dislike? Do you feel like you're a failure? Next, examine your *beliefs*. Do you think you're fat, unattractive, lazy, and unsuccessful? Admit to the negative beliefs you have of yourself. Lastly, what negative *behaviors* make up your way of being? Do you deny compliments? Have you noticed that you compare yourself to others? Do you stand in front of the mirror picking at certain body parts? Are you often focused on what you *haven't* achieved? Do you think back to how you *used* to be? Ask yourself these hard questions and make sure you write them down. Be honest with yourself, because your answers make up the unhealthy mindset responsible for your diet downfalls.

2. Discover the reasons for your negative feelings, beliefs, and behaviors.

Now it's time to ask *why* you are feeling, thinking, or behaving the way you are. Here is a personal example to help you dig deeper. When I had my first professional photo shoot, I was quite nervous about how the pictures would turn out. Despite all of the work I had done on myself prior to the shoot (hard workouts, strict diet, makeup, hair, etc.), I felt stressed that I wouldn't like my pictures. I battled my own body image issues about looking both old and chubby, picking at the parts of my body I disliked most. In order to change my negative feelings (stress and dislike), my negative beliefs ("I'm old and chubby") and my negative behavior (criticizing my body), it was important that I asked myself why I was thinking and doing these things. What I discovered was this: "I don't want to be a hypocrite in air-brushing my pictures when the purpose of my writing is to help women learn to love themselves. Therefore, I have to look perfect in order that I won't have to revert to air-brushing." Wow. Now isn't that an eye-opener? How do you think I'm doing with attempting to live up to my mindset of perfection? (Shockingly, not so great).

Now it's your turn. Take any negative feeling, belief, or behavior you identified in step one and ask yourself this simple question: *Why* am I feeling, thinking, or acting like this? Write down the first answers that come to mind. You may discover that digging deep to find the underlying reason is painful. However, once you've identified the true reasons you have a hard time accepting compliments, or why you compare yourself to others, or why you're focused on what you haven't achieved, you're on your way to healthy thinking and actually liking yourself!

3. Overcome your negative feelings, beliefs, and behaviors with a positive attitude.

You have identified the reasons behind your unhealthy feelings, beliefs, and behaviors – and these are all intertwined in a negative mindset cycle. For example, you may *feel* fat, which leads you to *believing* you're fat, so you choose to wear your "fat pants" today (your *behavior*). And let's say you discovered that the *reason* you feel fat is because you no longer feel attractive when you see how your clothes fit as you get dressed. Because you're aware of the contributing factors to your negative mindset cycle, you've now empowered yourself to transform it into a positive cycle of success! How do you do this? The key to mastering a healthy mindset is *intentionally changing your attitude*.

Your *attitude* is the answer to addressing your underlying reasons for your feelings, beliefs, and behaviors. You truly can overcome negative thinking and behavioral patterns, and eradicate your reasons for them, simply by changing your attitude! This is actually simple to do, but I warn you that it's not always easy – because you're actively reversing an unhealthy way of being. Therefore, you must decide to have a positive attitude – and renew this decision every single day. A great new attitude is one such as this: "I am a strong, beautiful woman, in control of my cravings, on a journey to a healthier me."

So, if you feel fat, believe you're fat, and want to wear your "fat pants" today because you hate how your clothes fit, it's time to combat this unhealthy mindset by negating it with your new attitude: "I'm on a journey to a healthier me so I refuse to get upset that my clothes don't fit right now. I will still dress attractively and accept compliments from others because I know that, despite needing to lose weight, I am still beautiful." You must be committed to talking to yourself like this! You absolutely cannot allow negative thoughts to linger in your mind. This will take practice but, just as you must commit to eradicating unhealthy foods from your cupboard to succeed at weight loss, you mustn't allow your negative feelings and beliefs to make a home in your mind's cupboard – or negative behaviors will be the inevitable result. Seek to replace your unhealthy mindset with a healthy, positive attitude, and every day it will get easier for you to daily choose the right thoughts about yourself.

You now have the answer to long-term weight-loss success: Lose your mind! That is, rid yourself of your negative mindset by maintaining a positive attitude. In order to reverse the negative effects of your ingrained feelings, beliefs, and behaviors that led to the unhealthy external you, you must be willing to do the work of transforming the internal you. This isn't a fad, or some heady, foo-foo, sit-in-the-lotus-position-and-chant type of stuff. Truly, if you want to have the health and body of your dreams, you must ensure your mindset is healthy. In fact, you'll discover that when you're focused on changing your inside, your outside will change! More importantly, you'll maintain the change because your new attitude has become a part of your way of being. Remember, you are what you believe you are. By cementing into your mind that you're strong, beautiful, self-controlled, and on a health journey that's making you better every day, you WILL get better! Not only will you fuel your thoughts to continue on the positive cycle of success, your perception of your body will constantly improve.

Once you have a positive perception of your body, it will inevitably transform into what you've always wanted it to become.

About Priscilla

Priscilla Freed is an entrepreneur, fitness expert, life coach, speaker, author, and wellness business mentor.

After graduating from UC Berkeley, Priscilla discovered that her carefree college diet of pizza and chocolate chip cookies left her with an expanded waistline and an unhealthy body image. Realizing that most women have similar struggles, Priscilla made it her mission to help women "lose their minds." She became a Certified Personal Trainer and Certified Life Coach, as well as received a Masters in Philosophy from Denver Seminary, where she first developed her mind-body program.

In 2006, Priscilla founded Holistic Health Corp, a whole-life coaching company whose mission is to radically change a woman's mindset in order to transform her body. Based in Littleton, Colorado, her company offers a number of local and virtual nutrition, fitness, and life coaching programs dedicated to changing women's lives. Priscilla is also the creator and director of Camp MissFits®, an award-winning fitness training program that brings together a top-notch coaching team with a Motley Crew of Motivated Women™. Priscilla's education and coaching experience in mindset, body image, fitness, and nutrition is the reason her holistic coaching programs help women achieve lifelong success.

Priscilla has been seen on 9News and Fox31's Colorado's Best, as well as in the Denver Business Journal, Denver Daily News, Littleton Independent, and the Denver Post. Also known as Sergeant Silla for her "no excuses" approach, Priscilla has motivated thousands of women to ACT in order to realize their greatest dreams.

To learn more about Priscilla Freed, her life-changing coaching programs, and how you can receive her free "Total Body-Mindset Makeover" training guide, visit: www.sergeantsilla.com or call: 303-220-0141.

CHAPTER 7

How Do You Get Great Results In A Traditional Gym? – Ignore What They Traditionally Tell You!

By Nick Osborne

Congratulations on your desire to lose your fat, get in better shape, and become healthier! A lot of people out there want a better body, but few are willing to take action. Not only are you ready to take action, but you are also seeking out good information to make sure you are going to do this more effectively and efficiently. Give yourself a pat on the back!

Now that you are finished back patting, let's get to work on getting the results you want. You've joined a gym. Are you instantly healthier? Of course not, but do you know what to do next? Of course you don't, and that's where the traditional gym deserts you.

I want to introduce you to Annie W. Oman. She represents anyone who is looking to lose body fat and get into shape, but doesn't have access to a great training and results-oriented gym like GO: Fitness in Columbus, Ohio. I want to help her (and you) get your better body AND your money's worth out of almost any other gym out there.

The challenge Annie will have is she is going to need to ignore most everything she hears or sees in the big box club's advertisements, posters and what she is shown in the gym.

Why? Well, let's face facts. Most gyms are interested in selling her a membership. They want to make getting in shape look easy and that it takes no effort. They are selling her what she wants to hear with words like "Fun" and "Easy."

The first hurdle Annie is usually going to encounter is being shown around by a 20-something-year-old hard-body salesperson, who has never had to work hard to keep his/her figure up. That person's body is not an endorsement of the gym and its effectiveness. That salesperson is younger with a higher metabolism and loves working and working out at the gym all day. Annie doesn't have that kind of time and lifestyle, yet is told subliminally that she too can look good by just simply joining.

Don't believe the hype. Why not? More than 90% of people who simply join commercial gyms never get the results they want. Here's the truth. If the traditional gyms told people what they really needed to do to get results; then more people who joined would get results… but less people would actually join.

That's what this chapter is designed to do. Help Annie, and you, avoid the mistakes people make when looking to join a traditional commercial gym. This section answers: "How do I get results in a traditional gym?"

YOU CAN'T OUTWORK A BAD DIET!

Annie is a woman in her mid 30 - 40s and has about 40 pounds she would like to lose. Imagine if right away the salesperson tells her, "Ma'am, I know you are wanting to join here to get into shape, but let me tell you, if you are not going to eat better, joining this gym will do little for you."

Would she be shocked? Of course she would, anyone would,…honesty from a salesperson?…What will they think of next? There are very few (if any) workouts so effective that you don't have to eat right to get results. Anywhere from 40% to 60% of the results you want are going to come from how, what, why, where and when you eat.

However, most gyms never tell you that.

Instead, Annie is lead to believe that being a member of this gym will almost guarantee results. Here's the catch. Traditional gyms leave the healthy diet plan up to her to discover on her own. Some gyms even bank on her getting so frustrated that she leaves (but still has to pay her dues), or they ask her for some outrageous fee for specialized diet planning.

Annie's gym should provide some sort of dietary guidance that is based on *real* eating with *real* foods for her *real-life*. However, since she won't get that from most gyms, she needs to find software that she can use and makes sense to her.

Annie's software should track her diet meal-by-meal and snack-by-snack. If it doesn't, then she needs to get a notebook and track this all day. Now, tracking all of this might seem like a giant pain in the rear, but she will be surprised at how effective writing down everything that she puts in her mouth is.

Tracking will make her aware of how often and how much she eats. Once Annie starts tracking her eating habits, she'll be astounded at how much fat starts to come off because Annie will become more conscious of what she's putting in her mouth. Awareness is her biggest tool when it comes to her diet. It will strengthen her ability to make better decisions on a daily basis, moment by moment. Few gyms will tell her that.

RUNNING, RUNNING, AND RUNNING, AND NOT GOING ANYWHERE OR GETTING RESULTS

Annie is now on the tour of the facility of XYZ Fitness. One of the first things that most gyms will show her is the endless supply of fancy treadmills, elliptical, stair-climbers, bikes and who-knows-what-else-types of cardio equipment. The problem with all of this new-fangled cardio equipment is that the way they will tell her to use it really won't help her to lose body fat, or give her the nice, toned, firm look that she wanted from the gym.

If boring, steady-state cardio helped you to reach your goals, then every single person who finished a marathon would have an incredible body. However, more than half of people who finish marathons are still considered overweight! That's right. The only thing those thousands of miles have done is teach their bodies how to burn almost no fat off of their bodies. That's kind of discouraging, right?

Now, don't get me wrong, if you're sedentary and just starting to work out, then a brisk walk will end up being a good beginning cardio workout for you. However, after you have attained a certain level of fitness, you need to shorten your cardio time and make it a bit more intense. You should include walking up hills, walking then slightly jogging, or eventually sprinting at a quicker pace, or anything else that might have you working in short bursts of high-energy activity.

So, why do gyms sell you on treadmills? Because you don't know any better, and because walking or jogging on a treadmill is easy to do with little or no education or training on the gym's part. Not to mention, they look new and flashy. It's also easier to sell you the new fancy cardio equipment than it is to teach you how to do a proper workout.

Treadmills and cardio equipment can be used effectively if you're going for short burst interval training. Highly effective cardio workouts for fat-loss and fitness should be completed in 20-25 minutes, including your warm up and cool down.

Shorter cardio times for better workouts can seem counterintuitive. Most people have been told the longer the better when it comes to cardio. The problem is, the longer you work out on a treadmill, the less intense your workout is. Science has proven intensity and frequency is more important than the duration of the workouts.

Why don't gyms tell you to do this? Because it's difficult! The most effective type of cardio should be really hard, intense and 'really suck' for 12 to 18 minutes. When doing cardio workouts, you should be able to walk into the gym, get changed, warm-up, do your cardio, and leave in 35 minutes or less.

This is more than enough activity for getting results and building fitness into your daily routine. Now, you can't just do interval training without some instruction or education, but most gyms don't tell you about that either. They just want to sell you lines of cardio equipment with small fans, TVs, hand massagers and arm rests and leave you be.

GET OFF THE STRENGTH MACHINES

The next thing Annie is going to be shown is the traditional weight-machine area. This is where they try to dazzle her again with more pretty machines. These machines are almost works of art, sculptures to modern day fitness. They appear easy and fun to use, and will whip her into shape, with little or no effort on her part.

The conversation might end up like this;

Salesperson: "Look how easy it is to workout on our machines".

Annie: "Easy? I thought lifting weights and getting stronger would be hard work."

Salesperson: "Not here at XYZ Fitness! Our machines make it effortless."

And in some regards they are right.

Most people don't know that weight machines were built for bodybuilders and rehab patients. They are a good change up, and might even be good the first few weeks you are working out, but they build strength you can't really use. In the real world, Annie doesn't get to lift things on machines that are balanced and stabilized for her. She doesn't do most of her lifting seated. So, why should her workouts be much different?

Your workouts should be hard. Which makes more sense to your life? Lying on a machine and leg pressing 200 pounds, or squatting down and picking up two 40-pound dumbbells off the floor. One is real strength you can use, and the other only looks good on their machines. DON'T BUY THEIR MACHINES!

IGNORE THE POSTERS AND BECOMING THE HULK!

When Annie walked into the gym or even before she got there, she has been inundated with images of in-shape women using eight or ten-pound dumbbells doing bicep curls and some sort of triceps exercise. This teaches women what kind of weights they should be using to get these awesome bodies. It tells them, "If you want toned arms, but you don't want to get too big and bulky, lift light weights." Isn't 'light weights' a contradiction?

Now, I've been in the fitness industry for more than 25 years, and my answer is always the same: Women can NOT get bulky. I've seen the science, and prove it everyday. Less than 2% of women have the possibility or genetic makeup to add large amounts of muscle mass. The average fit woman would need to work out four days a week, eating a perfect diet, and lifting ridiculous amounts of weight during each workout for more than an hour to add between five and 10 pounds of muscle in a year.

What usually happens, however, is that a woman starts lifting weights, and after two to five weeks, her clothes, skin and joints start to feel tight and stiff. So, she concludes she is one of the 1% to 2% of women that add muscle and get bulky like a female Hulk.

What is actually happening at this point is her body is storing more glycogen in its muscles. When you store more glycogen, you store a lot more water with that glycogen in the muscles. This leads to the muscles being slightly swollen for a short time, causing her skin and clothes to feel tighter than before she started her lifting program.

When this happens, most women stop lifting weights and go back to getting on the treadmill thus getting rid of their body's need to store sugars, and giving up the opportunity of really changing her body.

If she would just keep lifting intensely for another two to three weeks, her body would start getting rid of most of the excess water and glycogen. This will allow Annie to have those toned arms and legs as well as have enough muscle density to burn body-fat around the clock.

So, skip the 10s and 12s and start getting into the 20s and 25s as soon as you can. Stick it out through the "Inflationary Period" and you will be leaner and stronger when your body releases all the excess sugars and water.

CARDIO WEIGHT TRAINING (WHAT THE....?)

Here is something that Annie is rarely or never going to hear of in most commercial gyms, Cardio Lifting. Sometimes people confuse cardio or metabolic weight training with plain 'old fashioned' circuit training. Some gyms also call this metabolic circuit training, as what we call it at GO: Fitness. The difference between traditional circuit training, and metabolic circuit training or metabolic cardio lifting is this:

Traditional circuit training has you doing 3 or 4 exercises in a row with a certain number of reps and rest until you're ready for the next exercise. An example of this type of training would have you do 12 reps of chest press, squats, pull-ins and then crunches. Each one of these circuits could end up taking five minutes or longer because rest is not determined.

However, when doing metabolic cardio lifting, you could do the same exercises, with the same number of repetitions per set, but you're going to see how many rounds of the circuit you can do in eight minutes. So instead of getting one circuit done in four to six minutes and completing only two rounds, you lighten the weights by 15% and attempt to get four to six circuits done in eight minutes, with little or no rest between exercises or circuits.

Studies have shown that this type of lifting not only increases your cardiovascular system efficiency and health, but also optimizes hormones in your body to burn fat as well as getting the most out of the body's fat burning for the next 18 to 36 hours.

DO WHAT GYMS TELL YOU AND YOU ARE GOING TO GET BORED REALLY QUICK

If Annie thought for a moment, one thing she would realize is, if she stuck only to cardio equipment and machines, within 30 to 60 days she is going to be bored out of her mind. The gym never tells her this.

Wouldn't it be more professional if the gym told her she was going to have to pay for some advanced instruction?

Once you're in shape, it's well worth your time and money to invest in learning how to use kettlebells, ropes, TRX® (suspension training), BOSU®s, rubber bands and medicine balls. This will keep you from getting bored and continue seeing results long after the people that joined the gym the same day that you did. They are at home sitting on the couch eating potato chips, and still paying for their membership.

Don't think that "FREE CLASSES" with membership is going to solve your boredom problem. A lot of gyms offer these classes and claim they are your answer to cardio and lifting, circuit training and boredom. They have really cool names, sound awesome and seem as though they will help you reach your goals. The problems with these classes are:

1. They are so choreographed that it takes you weeks to know what dance step you need to do.

2. Yes, you are sweating, but you are not building your metabolism and optimizing your hormones, so you are not burning fat after you leave the gym.

3. There is little or no instruction, direction and feedback given because the class is so large and taught by an "Aerobics" person who is getting in their own workout, and is not truly focused on you.

4. Nationally, the injury rate within the first 90 days of beginning these free classes is over 50%. Annie is very likely to get injured and/or waste her time with these classes. (Did they forget to tell that to her on her tour of the gym?) You need to work to your level, and classes over 12 people

make it really hard to give any one person longer than about 4 minutes of personalized instruction per hour.

BEING SOCIAL ISN'T ALWAYS GOOD

One of the common sales strategies that will be used with Annie on her tour is to talk about how social this gym is, and to talk about how many members there are to build up the idea of making friends at the gym.

Whether she is bringing her friends in or making new friends in the gym, she needs to make sure they are there to help her reach her goals, and not distract her. The people that she is working out with are going to be there to help hold her accountable and to make it enjoyable to go work out, but not stand in her way of an effective and efficient workout.

This means you and your "buddies" might show up at the same time, encourage each other, and hold each other accountable. However, you don't talk during your workout. Chatting during your workout is not going to allow you to work out hard and fast.

If chatting in the gym either cuts down on the number of repetitions that you're doing or increases the length of time you're in the gym, then these social times are actually going to keep you from getting the results you want fast enough and frustrate you. You won't lose the muffin top, but you gained a pal for a few times a week.

Why did you join the gym again? Get some social support, but keep it light and all about the workouts. Friends don't let friends stay out of shape (fat).

SUMMING IT ALL UP

You can be successful in a traditional, commercial gym if you are smart, and don't fall for everything they say. You just need to ignore most everything they tell you and attempt to sell you.

Follow these suggestions and you will achieve your goals quickly and enjoy your time in the gym, without getting sucked into lots of supplements, additional charges or buying equipment or things you don't need.

To get the results you want, put your headphones on, work hard, work quickly, work regularly and focus on yourself!

About Nick

Nick Osborne has been in the fitness industry for more than 25 years. He's been a part of every aspect of the gym business from desk person, membership sales person, head personal trainer, all the way to owner of two clubs (one fitness center and one sports performance center).

Nick has seen all the fads come and go and focuses on building systems and methods that get people fast results in a fun and effective way. He created his gym to be one of the most effective training gyms in the Midwest by providing fun workouts and training his coaches up to 12 times longer than any of his competitors.

The secret to his gym's success is not just the exercises, but more so how the coaches and staff work with clients. His coaches focus on every aspect of the clients' lives that can affect them getting the results they want. His systems also provide nutrition education, cardio workouts and metabolic circuit training, as well as foam rolling and stretching programs to each and every client.

Nick's system is so effective for the club, coach and client, that gyms and fitness centers around the world have sought him out for consulting, public speaking and to implement his system into their gyms. Nick used his **"Integrated Functional Coaching System®"** to train himself to win 14 U.S. titles in full-contact and traditional Kung Fu, and a World Championship in Traditional Kung Fu, and he is the only person to win N.A.S.S.'s North America's Strongest Man twice.

The IFCS has also been used in training professional athletes, World's Strongest Man champion, Phil Pfister, The Ohio State University varsity football, wrestling and field hockey teams, as well as more than 10,000 people around the world – to get the bodies they want.

To learn more about Nick Osborne and his training center, you can visit the gym's website: www.GoFitnessCenter.com or call 614-481-8080.

If you want more information on his training system for gyms, visit: www.PersonalTrainingDepartmentBlueprint.com or call 614-453-1786.

CHAPTER 8

Interval Training

By Leks Stanic & Dewayne Holifield

[Disclaimer: This chapter was created to help you reach your fitness goals and it was created for the general public. Therefore, it is highly recommended that you get your physician's approval before beginning any exercise program. These recommendations are for educational purposes only. It is your responsibility to consult your physician before starting any exercise program. It is important you do so especially if you have any medical condition or injury that may get worse due to any physical activity. This program is designed for healthy individuals 18 years of age and older.

You are taking full responsibility for your safety. Before practicing in the exercise programs contained in this chapter, do not take risks beyond your level of experience, ability, training and fitness.
Do not perform any exercise without proper instruction. Always do a dynamic warm-up prior to strength training and/or interval training. See your physician before starting any exercise and/or nutrition program. If you experience any lightheadedness, dizziness, or shortness of breath while exercising, stop exercising immediately and consult your physician.

It is also highly recommended that you have a complete physical examination once a year regardless of health status, but especially if you are sedentary, if you have high cholesterol, high blood pressure, and/or diabetes, if you are overweight, or if you are over 30 years old and/or have any other medical problem. Any changes made to nutritional plans should be discussed with a physician or a registered dietitian. Your physician's recommendations and orders are always above the content of this book.]

'INTERVAL TRAINING'

Interval training has become one of the biggest fitness crazes in the fitness industry today. It has taken the fitness world by storm because it is far superior to any other method of training for someone who is trying to achieve overall fitness (strength & endurance, cardiovascular components of fitness).

Have you ever gone to a car dealership and looked at the sticker for a luxury vehicle and it shows "18 mpg on the highway and 12 mpg in the city"? Have you ever wondered why highway mileage is always better than city mileage? Here's why: Vehicles use computers to adjust to steady speeds to use less fuel. It is more difficult to do this while operating a vehicle in the city due to all the stop-and-go. Now what in the world does this have to do with interval training? Well that actually represents how interval training works with our bodies.

Our body uses carbohydrates and fats for fuel. When we workout, our goal is to make the body use as much fat as it can. Having said that, if you do steady state cardio (for example, running or riding a bike, same resistance, same speed for an extended period of time), your body will adjust the rate at which it burns fuel (as stated above carbohydrates, fat and other micronutrients stored in the body for energy) at a steady pace, burning just enough calories needed to take you through the workout. And as soon as you are done with such a steady-state workout, you stop burning extra calories almost immediately. However, if you were to stop-and-go, you would burn significantly more calories overall than steady-state as your body cannot adjust to a stop-and-go. It has to constantly burn more calories trying to catch up with oxygen intake (also known as "oxygen debt") and energy depletion. And it takes much more effort to start moving, then come to a stop and to start all over again, rather than continuing at the same pace (thanks, inertia!). When it comes to "catching up on oxygen," many studies and much research has shown that we still burn significantly more calories even after the workout has ceased because of that particular (interval) workout. You will find anywhere between 16 to 38 hrs. after a workout that you have increased your metabolic rate. Obviously that rate declines the more time passes by, but it's amazing that you're still burning more calories even 12 hrs. after a workout just because of the type of workout you have done! This is also why rest is important, because with interval training, it is easy to overtrain if you do this every day. Take a day of rest in between if you feel tired. Listen to your body.

Why is interval training superior to the traditional steady-state cardio exercises that have been recommended in the past? Well, the answer is multi-fold. First of all, it provides a more intense workout by raising your heart rate substantially. When the heart rate increases during an intense interval, there is a huge demand for ventricular output. That means your muscles are demanding more blood and oxygen to support the intensity of the interval. The demand for oxygen uptake directly affects one's VO2Max, which is a prime component in measuring cardiovascular fitness.

We have all heard about how to train "from the book" – we've all heard somewhere along the way that we should go to the gym, and then do 3 sets of a particular exercise, 12-15 reps each, rest in between, move to the next exercise. Soon when you start training like this, you find out it's not that simple. What exercises should I do? How do you divide body parts? What order should I do those exercises in? Is that the ultimate workout for my particular fitness goals? How much should I rest between sets? Does it matter how much I rest? How do I know how much weight to use? How do I know when to increase the weight? How much time should I spend at the gym? Is a treadmill enough? Should I add cardio? Should I just do weights? Should I do cardio before or after the weights? These are all typical questions people ask trainers as if it could be answered so simply. But people just don't know those answers, as they are just confused with too much information. This is why we have decided to pair up with trainers from all over the US and give you each of our perspectives all in one book. Here you can find a workout that fits you personally. And hopefully you can find all the answers to your questions.

Now to answer all those questions above, we have found that interval training covers most of those questions in one type of workout. This is why we find it superior to other ways of training when it comes to overall fitness. Again, if you are trying to only increase your size by gaining muscle, this workout doesn't fit your needs. This is for those that are trying to increase their cardiovascular capacity, lower body fat percentage, tone up, get a "tighter" body, and be healthier overall – without spending too much time at a fitness facility.

Interval training can be done in number of ways: body type specific, full body training, strength and cardio, etc. The ultimate interval training (in our opinion) is High Intensity Interval Training – also known as HIIT (sometimes shown as "Hit"). HIIT is the best because it can be done for such a short period of time (9-30 minutes, some people say no more than 20 mins.) with extremely good results. So, when it comes to HIIT, the name itself explains the intensity of the workout – you must use your energy to the maximum during this type of training (check the end of the chapter for a few sample workouts).

When talking about the different interval training protocols, you must first assess where you are in overall cardiovascular and muscular endurance fitness-wise. If you are doing interval training on your own or with a fitness professional, it is imperative that you understand that HIIT is going to be much more difficult than steady-state cardio. If your cardiovascular and muscular endurance are not the best, you may want to choose an interval protocol that allows you to perform exercises for 30 seconds and take a 1-minute rest. Once you find that you can perform a given movement (for example, bodyweight squats) at an all-out-effort and can recover in less than a minute, you can then adjust the amount of rest based on the reduction in measured recovery time. So, instead of a 30sec/1min interval protocol, you may see yourself adjusting to a 30sec/45sec interval protocol. As your VO2max increases, the amount of rest needed reduces.

Interval timing is not set in stone. You can adjust the work/rest ratio to whatever challenges you wish, as an individual and training on your own. However, in most group training sessions that are guided by a fitness professional, the work/rest ratio is set. Say for instance you participate for the first time in a boot camp at a local gym and there is a list of bodyweight exercises that you must perform at 30/30 (work/rest) ratio and as you begin to perform the exercises, you find yourself falling behind - short of breath and not able to keep up. Well, there is a way to perform these exercises within the times prescribed and still keep up. You must adjust your intensity level to a point to still make it challenging and complete the workout. Most fitness professionals refer to this as R.P.E (Rate of Perceived Exertion). So instead of going at 100%, or all out, you can adjust your level of intensity on "exertion" to say, 60 or 70%. As you get better and your VO2max has increased, you can increase the level of exertion to 85% and even 90% to challenge yourself. We have trained classes where the interval was 1 minute with no rest. We only give them enough time to transition to the next exercise. But obviously this workout was done with individuals who are ready for that level of workout – they can maintain form and perform an exercise at its max for that period of time. It is still very challenging for them, but they are able to complete the workout none-the-less.

Boot camp and small group training sessions that are conducted by a fitness professional are usually pretty intense. They usually last between 20 and 45 minutes. Most people can't go beyond that because the work/rest interval is usually designed to burn the most fat (fuel) in the shortest amount of time. We recommend when doing interval training that you use compound movements such as bodyweight squats, lunges, shoulder presses, burpees, 8-count body-builders, pushups, rowing type movement for your back, etc., by calling on the maximum amount of muscle with a maximum amount of intensity or RPE. You add a level of intensity that cannot be rivaled by any type of steady-state cardio.

You might have already heard of one type of interval training called Tabata training. It's based on 20/10 timing (meaning 20 seconds of work followed by 10 seconds of rest/transition to the next exercise) for the total of 4 minutes, totaling 8 rounds. However, as stated above, there is no need to limit yourself when it comes to timing and exercises. This is just one way of using training intervals. We like to change our timing frequently, and by doing that we're making it more fun and also making sure that the body doesn't get used to any type of workout. Sure you can always push yourself for more, but if you're going for overall health and weight-loss/toning goals, you always want to change it around for your body. If you do something repetitively, it's not a bad thing, but just keep in mind that you always need to push yourself and you should never allow the body to get "comfortable" with any workout. You can change the exercises, change the order of the exercises, add core workouts in between, change the timing.... you can get creative as long as you are challenging yourself with each workout.

Here are some examples of interval work/rest protocols: 20/10 (not for the "faint of heart"), 30/30, 30/15, 45/15, 60/0 (beast mode!!). Do not limit yourself to these ratios. Mix it up and always challenge yourself. The results you reap will be bountiful. This is why it's important to choose the exercises properly so that the timing actually makes sense. If you chose exercises that are too easy for you, then the interval training, no matter what timing you use, may be wasted. Let's put it this way – you should pretty much be on the floor when done with HIIT with just enough energy to cuss your trainer out☺.

WORKOUT SAMPLES

Workout A (Beginner workout):
30sec/rest till ready for next exercise up to 1min.

- Push-ups
- High knees (in place)
- Seated band back row
- Box (or step) step-ups
- Dumbbell shoulder press

Workout B:
40/20 protocol. After all 5 exercises are completed, take 1minute rest. Then repeat all 4 times. The total workout will be completed in 24 minutes –including rest time).

- Jumping jacks
- 8-count body builders
- Hello dolly or reverse crunch
- Push-ups
- Bent over band or DB row

Workout C:
20/10 protocol - 10 rounds (20mins.) (*This is not Tabata. It's only 20-10 protocol but not for 4 minutes straight. In this workout, you keep moving to the next exercise after each set for total of 20 minutes.)

- Plank w/hip raise or Russian medicine ball twist
- Long lunge (stationary, switch legs)
- Kettlebell swing (choose heavier Kettlebell. Make sure you know proper form).

- Bodyweight jump squat (when jumping gets too much for your legs, switch to regular squats – don't compromise the form)

*All these videos (and more) are available at: www.CPFitBody.com. Please visit for more information.

*You can apply any work/rest protocol to the above as long as you constantly challenge yourself.

About Leks

Leks Stanic, health and wellness expert, has formed CPFitBody after realizing how much false health information is provided to the public. Leks, who once lived unhealthy herself, has learned on her own about proper lifestyle, and discovered that anyone can benefit greatly from wellness programs. Leks has completed over ten fitness and specialty certifications through nationally recognized organizations such as NCSF, AFAA, Exercise, Etc. and IDEA. (You can visit CPFitBody.com for her 'before' and 'after' pictures.)

Leks' background consists of Strength & Conditioning, Track & Field and Muay Thai Kickboxing. She has worked with a wide range of people – from athletes to people with specific needs such as women with bone-loss issues to large group training.

Leks (along with Dewayne) currently runs CPFitBody studio located in Franklin, TN. CPFitBody offers private training, semi-private and small group classes.

For more information, please visit: www.CPFitBody.com

Also, for latest health and fitness tips, follow us on Twitter @CPFitBody and "Like" us on Facebook: Consistently Persistent Fitness.

About Dewayne

Fitness and health expert Dewayne Holifield is certified as a Strength and Conditioning Specialist though the National Federation of Personal Trainers.

Dewayne was in the US Navy, where he received military boot camp training and was a fitness coordinator with the Naval Communications Unit in Washington, DC. He has over 20 years of experience in the fitness industry and has been enriching the lives of individuals through health and fitness since 1990. He has extensive experience in boot camp style training, interval training, bodybuilding competition training, and sport-specific training.

Dewayne has impacted peoples' lives in a positive way from Gold's Gym, AC Fitness and World Gym in Birmingham, AL to Bally Total Fitness and Snap Fitness in Jacksonville, FL. He (along with Leks) currently runs CPFitBody in Franklin, TN.

For more information, please visit: www.CPFitBody.com

Also, for latest tips, follow us on Twitter @CPFitBody and "Like" us on Facebook: Consistently Persistent Fitness.

CHAPTER 9

How To Train, Eat And Look Like An Athlete In Three Simple Steps

By Callie Durbrow

Growing up I was an athlete; I played soccer, basketball, participated in karate and gymnastics and was generally active. I went on to play soccer and basketball in college. During that time my workout regime was pretty great. Being a soccer player I was lean and had great endurance. I lifted weights three times a week and was explosive and flexible at the same time. This all happened through no real planning of my own, I just trained like an athlete. I jumped, sprinted, lifted weights and trained in intervals by default on the soccer field.

After I graduated from college, I ran into what many former athletes do. What do I do with my competitive spirit now that I'm done playing sports? So, I did what many athletes that I knew were doing. I took up running.

It was a great way to pass the time and to "keep in shape," or so I thought. I was running a minimum of 3 miles per day, often times more. I was lifting weights, but not as regularly. What happened to my body in this time? Looking back it's very easy to see. I became slower, more flabby and soft (even though I didn't have a lot of body fat, I didn't look lean and athletic) and I had much less energy.

After a few years of working as a personal trainer, I was getting back into the gym, lifting weights and doing some different things with my nutrition. I was also taking a very close look at my clientele and what their situations were like.

As it turns out, the majority of people were coming in with very similar situations. Here is what most new clients were telling me:

I usually do cardio for about 30 to 45 minutes.

I don't do any strength training (this is usually because of feelings of intimidation, lack of knowledge or fear of getting bulky).

I weigh myself 3-4 times per week.

I eat cereal for breakfast, a sandwich for lunch and pasta for dinner.

I drink 2-3 cups of coffee every day and I drink 2 bottles of water.

I sleep 6 hours a night.

I work in an office or a lab for 8-9 hours each day.

These comments are taken directly from very real clients of mine. This may sound a bit like your lifestyle. You may be wondering what's wrong with this? If you are, then I'm excited for you because I'm about to open some doors to a lifestyle and a body shape that you never knew existed. You may also be thinking that you understand most of these things are incorrect when it comes to fat loss but you're not sure how to change them. I'm excited for you too, because you are going to embark on a thrilling journey of fat loss, body reconstruction and most importantly, lifestyle transformation.

I'm going to give you the three-step process a bit later in this section, but first we need to lay some groundwork. I'm not going to go into extreme detail about mindset because that's an entire book in itself. Instead I want you to start to understand that having the right mindset is critical for your success.

As an athlete we were always taught to visualize what you want. See your success before it happens. I had a business mentor who taught me to think about my life every single day as being my ideal life. Visualize, in detail, your success as though it's already in front of you. That's what I want you to do with your body and life transformation here. Sit down and visualize your ideal body. Think about exactly how you would like to look and get a crystal clear image of that. Also think about how you want your lifestyle to look. How do you want to feel every day? How do you want others to view you? How do you want to go through the day?

What emotions come up when you think about these things? Bookmark those in your mind, and think about them every day. Your subconscious cannot decipher whether these thoughts are your truth or simply just powerful thoughts. Do this exercise every day.

The second part of this process is to set goals. The best way to do this is to get your circumference measurements, body fat analysis and a 'before' photo done by a qualified fitness professional. You don't want to be a slave to the scale because this athletic lifestyle is all about body composition. You want to look lean and tight, not skinny and soft. Therefore your focus should be on losing body fat, losing inches and developing lean and toned muscle along the way.

You might weigh 130 pounds according to the scale but 130 pounds with 30% body fat (39 pounds of overall fat) will look a lot different than 130 pounds with 20% body fat (26 pounds of overall fat).

Taking a photo every 4-6 weeks will also enhance your confidence because sometimes it's hard to see those small changes; a few inches off the waist, better posture, more confidence. Those things all shine through in photos.

The last part of the method is to put it into action. I have a very simple way of getting my clients to take action. Schedule your training just like any other appointment. Whether you are going to the gym to meet your trainer or you're doing a conditioning workout on your own time, put it in your calendar. There is something very powerful about a schedule. If you can stay accountable to other people, that's an added bonus. That's why many of my clients have trained with me for

5-6 years. They love the results, but they also love the accountability.

Now, here is the meat of the program. The three-step process that I want you to follow is very simple:

1. Strength Training

2. Conditioning

3. Nutrition

I know what you're thinking, "...that's it?"

Well, yes and no. You need to make sure that you're following the three steps, but they have to be done correctly...in order to see the 'rockstar' changes that will undoubtedly occur.

1. STRENGTH TRAINING

Strength training is one of the best ways to reshape your body. This method will help you develop lean and toned muscle and simultaneously improve your metabolism (the rate at which your body burns calories) because muscle is a much more active tissue than fat.

The key to strength training for a 'rockstar body' is to perform full body workouts. These workouts will not only burn the highest amount of calories, but they will also rev your body up so that you're burning calories post-workout. Here are some key points for your strength training sessions:

- Perform multi-muscle movements, ones that work a large amount of muscles simultaneously

- Perform full body workouts

- Train 2-4 times per week

- Exercises such as squats, lunges, push ups, pull up variations, jumps, sprints and kettlebell work are the foundations of the program

- Perform every workout with perfect form

- Focus on the intensity of each workout. You want to get a ton of work done

2. CONDITIONING

I want you to notice that in this section I didn't say cardio. Cardio is an evil word in this plan, because it brings to the surface some mind-numbing workout on the elliptical trainer while watching reruns of the Kardashians. It's not only boring, but it's super ineffective if you want the 'rockstar body.'

Instead you need to focus on conditioning workouts. These are done in short bursts for an overall short amount of time to get more work done in less time and burn more calories. This usually sounds very appealing to people because you don't waste any precious time and it's very efficient in terms of the results.

Here's what your conditioning workouts should consist of:

- Short sessions, no more than 30 minutes (including warm-up and cool down).

- Focus on a short burst of work followed by a short rest and continued in that fashion until the workout is completed.

- Each short burst of work should be intense and all-out.

- The best methods are hill sprints, stadium sprints, jump rope, bike sprints, Prowler or sled push and pull, Battling Ropes and Burpees.

- An example of this type of workout would be: sprint up a moderate hill with all out effort. Walk back down and rest for 1 minute then repeat this for 8 to 10 sprints.

3. NUTRITION

Nutrition has been a mystical topic for many people. There are so many "diets" to choose from, no wonder everyone is confused and still holding onto too much body fat. As I kept the process simple, I'm going to keep the nutrition plan simple as well. The major focus of the 'rockstar nutrition plan' is to eat for performance and for desired body composition.

This plan is a modified low-carbohydrate focus with intermittent fasting. Sound confusing? It's really not. Intermittent fasting is simply planned periods of fasting followed by a "feeding window." Generally the best way to start is with a 16-hour fast followed by an 8-hour feeding window. You'll want to break your fast with a post-workout shake (unsweetened almond milk, 1 scoop of whey protein and frozen fruit blended). Then you'll have 3 other meals within that window. I typically recommend an 11:00 am to 7:00 pm feeding window but the great thing about this plan is that you can modify it to fit your lifestyle.

This type of eating plan has some great benefits:

- Decreased cravings and overall feelings of hunger that come about with a typical 2-3 hour eating plan
- Easy to follow with a busy lifestyle
- Improved fat burning potential because during the fasting phase the body is working to burn fat and not sugar stores
- By delaying breakfast you are allowing your body to continue to produce growth hormone (it's highest overnight and first thing in the morning) which helps the body develop muscle and burn fat
- Improved insulin sensitivity (how efficiently your body processes carbohydrates) which also contributes to faster fat loss

Here are your key points:

- Avoid all grains, bread, pasta, rice and cereal
- Get your carbohydrates from fruits (mainly berries), vegetables, post-workout shakes and sweet potatoes

- Eat protein with every meal and snack
- Break your fast with your post-workout shake
- Eat 3 more times during the feeding window on days that you train with weights
- Eat 2 more times during the feeding window on days that you rest or perform conditioning workouts

Calorie intake will vary but here's a general rule of thumb:

Take your body weight and multiply by 10. That's a rough estimate of the number of calories you should be taking in per day. So if you weigh 140, you'll be taking in about 1400 calories. On days that you don't train with weights or on off days, drop this number by 200-300. This basically means cutting out your post-workout shake on rest days or having a lower calorie version on days you perform sprints or conditioning.

Now that you have your mindset, your scheduling abilities and your three points of focus for a 'rockstar body', it's time to put it all together and execute.

Here's an example of a weekly training schedule:
Monday - Full body strength
Tuesday - Hill sprints
Wednesday - Rest
Thursday - Full body strength
Friday - Jump rope circuit
Saturday - Full body strength
Sunday - Rest

Here are some sample full-body workouts:
Workout #1
Perform each exercise in a circuit fashion with minimal rest. Rest 1:30 after each circuit and repeat for 5 rounds.

- Kettlebell Swings x15
- Push Up (variations) x15

- Body Rows or TRX Rows x10-12
- Walking Lunges x30
- Valslide Body Saws x15
- Side Planks x15/side

Workout #2

Perform each exercise for 30 seconds followed by 15-second rest/transition. Rest 1 minute between circuits and repeat for 5 rounds.

- Jump Squats
- Push Ups
- Single Leg Box Squats (start on non-dominant leg)
- Medicine Ball Slams
- Kettlebell Swings
- Physio Ball Ab-Rollout

Here are some sample conditioning workouts:

Hill Sprints — find a hill that takes you 15-25 seconds to sprint up. Sprint at maximum effort to the top, walk down and then rest 1 minute. Repeat for 8-10 sprints depending on your fitness level.

Jump Rope circuit — jump rope for 1 minute, recover for 1 minute and repeat this cycle for a total of 20 minutes.

Bike Sprints — this can be done on a stationary or spin bike at the gym. Warm up for 3 minutes with no resistance. Crank up the resistance and sprint for 30 seconds. Recover with no resistance for 1 minute and repeat that cycle (minus the warm-up) for a total of 20 minutes. Perform a cool-down ride for 3 minutes.

The 'rockstar body plan' is a lifestyle change. You won't see any quick fixes in this program. It's a simple method using three basic principles but as you can see, some of the aspects are going away from the norm. What I've learned over the years is that in order to see amazing success you must stray from what everyone else is doing and step out of your comfort zone to make a change. If you continue to do what you've always done, you'll get the same result.

Focus on small changes each week in the areas of nutrition, workout intensity and mindset. Keep up with your measurements and photos to reinforce your success and enjoy the process. This is part of a journey to revealing your highest potential. Most people never realize just how great they can look because they don't have the right tools to truly succeed. This is your chance to break out of the typical cycle of achieving minimal results and success. Rock out this program and create the 'rockstar body' that you deserve!

About Callie

Callie Durbrow is the owner of Durbrow Performance Training in Cambridge, Massachusetts and is one of the most sought-after trainers in the Boston area. Her training methods have helped hundreds of local clients lose fat and inches and boost their energy levels using the simple 3-in-1 fat blasting formula. Clients avoid cardio, fad diets and traditional gym workouts and instead focus on resetting their metabolism, conditioning workouts and strength training.

Callie has been featured in Blast Magazine, Elite FTS, The Cambridge Chronicle, Wicked Local Somerville, The Improper Bostonian, Personal Fitness Professional Magazine and on NESN.

She is also the author of "*Breakthrough Metabolism*," a cutting edge guide to fast fat loss on Amazon.com.

To learn more about Callie Durbrow and her training methods, please visit:
http://www.durbrowperformance.com
http://www.ultimateathleticfitness.com.
Or, call: 800.668.7984.

CHAPTER 10

Change Your Life Through Fitness With 10 Easy Steps

By Sean Millhouse

I'm often asked who my best success story is. In 14 years, I have had quite a few that I could share:

–clients that have lost 100+ pounds

–people who have completed their first marathon and

–moms that were finally able to lose the "baby weight"

But I believe my absolute best (and favorite) client success story has to be Mary.

When I first heard Mary's story, she was an absolute mess. Mary's life had taken control of her. She was a single mother working a full-time job during the day, and taking care of her ailing parents at night. Mary spent her days as a nurse taking care of patients that were too sick to take care of themselves. And when Mary made it home, she took care of her 12 year old daughter and elderly parents. On a good night, she had a few minutes to herself to sit down and watch some mindless television. During the weekend, Mary would spend the entire day with her daughter doing whatever sounded fun.

Mary's life became so hectic that she had absolutely no time for herself to exercise, read or take a vacation. And at some point, cooking was replaced with fast food on most nights. She was so busy taking care of others, she didn't have time to take care of herself. Mary had gained 30 pounds in less than 3 years. She was not fitting into her clothes, she was depressed, and she was tired of feeling tired. Mary knew she needed to change something, but she didn't know where to start. She needed help!

During our initial consultation, Mary and I both agreed that the path she was on was not healthy for her or her loved ones. She had come to a cross-road. I explained to her that her fitness journey would not be easy. But I promised her that it would be worth every step of the way. The following 10 Steps are how we changed Mary's life through Fitness. You too can follow the same steps and enjoy the life-changing benefits.

1. TAKE A LOOK IN THE MIRROR

Before you can address a problem, you have to know what the problem is. Some people walk through life overweight, out of shape and/or unhealthy and they are perfectly ok with it. Good for them (I guess). However, most people that I know and meet are not happy with something about their health and fitness. There is some facet in their health and fitness that they want to change. This step is really something that only you can do yourself. What part of your health and fitness do you want to change?

In Mary's case, her life was out of control. She did not want to buy bigger clothes, she wanted to get off her depression medication and she wanted to start feeling good again. Mary woke up one day and just said enough was enough. She wanted to lose weight, start eating healthier and incorporating an exercise program. But she didn't know where to start. That's when she came to the conclusion that she needed help.

2. HIRE A FITNESS COACH

Have you ever noticed that all the best athletes in the world have a coach? Think about that for a second. Athletes that are already excellent at their sport know that it is critical to have a coach to help make them even better. So, if you want to make a change in your health and fitness, you should hire a fitness coach.

When Mary hired me as her fitness coach, she was a little reluctant. She didn't know what a fitness coach was supposed to do. I explained to Mary that a great fitness coach would be what she needed him/her to be. Some days she may need a cheerleader and other days it might need to be a teacher. I shared with her that the best fitness coaches will be there every step of the way for her. I let Mary know that before I started creating her program, we have to sit down and do a complete fitness assessment.

3. RIP OFF THE BAND-AID

Now that you are aware of your problem(s) and you have found your guide in your health and fitness journey, it's time to do some assessments. If you want to get directions to a destination, you have to know where you are at now. Your health and fitness are no different. There are several different fitness assessments that can be performed to get you a good idea of where you are. Some of my favorites are:

- Functional Movement Screen (to assess quality of movement)
- Blood Pressure
- Bodyweight
- Body Fat percentage
- Body Composition
- Endurance Test
- Strength Test

During my assessment of Mary, I took her Blood Pressure, Bodyweight, Body Fat percentage, Body Composition and Strength Test. Here were her results:

- BP: 139/87
This is a borderline high reading. I encouraged her to visit with her doctor to get a history established.

• Bodyweight: 217 lbs.
I'm not a big fan of taking bodyweight as a stand-alone measurement. However, this is definitely high for a 43 year old female who is 5'3"

• Body Fat Percentage: 39.3%
This is high for a female of any age. I usually like to see it at 20-25%.

• Body Composition:
131.7 lbs of lean muscle, bone and tissue. When you are starting an exercise program, this number should go up a little or at the very least be maintained. I never want to see this number go down as you lose weight.

85.3 lbs of Fat. This number definitely needs to come down.

• 0 Push-ups and 13 crunches in 60 seconds
These results are poor. They indicate that Mary is deconditioned.

4. DEFINE SUCCESS

To achieve success in anything you do in life, you have to define what success is. With your health and fitness program you should make clear goals of what you want to accomplish. For some people, that might be losing 75 lbs, for others it may be to bench press 300 lbs one time. It could even be a simple goal of walking up two flights of steps without getting out of breath. The point is, you need to be as specific as possible. It is also a good idea to put a deadline on your goal. Again, be specific.

With Mary, we decided to focus on one number: Body Fat Percentage. I explained to her that if this number went in the right direction, everything else should follow. We set a goal of getting below 25% in 9 months. Losing more than a 1/3 of her Body Fat sounded like an insurmountable task. So we broke it down into smaller goals. Her monthly goal was to lose 1.5%, and that's it. That is a very realistic and doable goal. Mary finally had a glimmer of hope...now she wanted to know how to do it.

5. MAKE A FITNESS PLAN

Having a goal without a plan is like rowing across the Atlantic Ocean to England without a paddle. You need to have the tools to get you there. A health and fitness plan can be 'super simple' or extremely complicated – depending on your goals and current fitness level. For someone trying to improve their endurance, it may be as simple as tracking your caloric intake and walking 10,000 steps in a day. For an elite athlete, it may get as involved as how many hours a day to train, refueling the body on a very strict schedule and getting a certain amount of sleep. But all fitness plans have the same 4 basic components: Strength Training, Endurance Exercise, Supportive Nutrition and Recovery/Flexibility.

For Mary we came up with the following initial fitness plan:

(i). Strength Training – Mary was to complete 2 days per week (Monday and Thursday) of a total body strength training circuit. She did 2 sets of 10 repetitions on 7 different exercises in a circuit fashion. It took approximately 15-20 minutes to complete. She did this immediately after work before she went home.

(ii). Endurance Exercise – She was instructed to walk at a brisk pace for an hour total (20 minutes before work, 20 minutes during lunch, and 20 minutes after work) on Tuesday, Wednesday and Friday. When she was finished with the strength circuit, she was given an interval bicycle workout for 16 minutes. She alternated pedaling with more resistance (level 10) for 1 minute and pedaling with less resistance (level 3) for 1 minute.

(iii). Supportive Nutrition – Mary was asked to start journaling her food and fluid intake. I asked her to write down the time she was eating, amounts of each food and amount of fluid intake. I showed her how to use an online calorie counter so that she could start consuming between 1600-1800 calories per day. We spent a lot of time going over making healthier choices.

(iv). Recovery/Flexibility – I came up with five pre-workout "warm-up" exercises for Mary to perform before each strength training session. In addition, I showed her a series of static and dynamic stretches as well as foam roll exercises to complete after each exercise day. We also discussed the importance of getting regular sleep each night to allow her body to recover properly.

6. TAKE ACTION

This is the step that loses a lot of people. You have done all the hard work in making the plan, now you just have to implement it. Make a commitment to yourself that you WILL do this for the next month... no excuses. Creating new habits is how you will succeed. To borrow a phrase from Nike: **Just Do It!**

This is the step where Mary excelled! She was like a race car that just had to be pointed in the right direction. Once I gave her the plan, she was like clock-work from week 1. This is the point when I knew Mary was going to succeed – no matter what.

7. RE-EVALUATE

Everyone wants to see progress when they are working hard. A very important part of the process is to Re-Evaluate and track your progress. I recommend re-measuring every 4-6 weeks. Did you improve these past several weeks? Or did you stay the same...or worse, back track? In either scenario, it's critical to know.

I remember going into Mary's first re-evaluation. She was certain that she hadn't made any progress. Remember, Mary's first goal was to lose 1.5% in her first month. Guess what: she shattered it! Mary dropped 3.2% bodyfat. She was high on life! I was so proud of her, and you could see she was proud of herself. These results further motivated her to keep going.

8. WEATHER THE COURSE

Every great plan has to be flexible and every motivated person has a hurdle to overcome. Maybe it's too hot to walk outside. Then you have to modify your plan. Maybe you join a gym or buy a treadmill. But you don't stop. You may have a bad day or week, and you miss a workout or two. Don't get down on yourself! You have to get right back on track.

For Mary, time was her biggest hurdle. During her 3rd month she only dropped 0.7% bodyfat. As you recall she had several people that depended on her care (her 12 year old and elderly parents). Mary was finding that working out after getting off work was proving to be a big challenge. So we adapted her program a bit. She actually found that it was easier to get up early and go to the gym before work. So we changed her program to be completed before work and during lunch. Mary loved it…and flourished!

9. REAP THE REWARDS

Everyone wants to feel good about themselves. People like to be rewarded for their hard work. So I think it's a great idea to come up with some good rewards for yourself as you improve your health and fitness. Maybe it's a new wardrobe, a massage, or a new pair of running shoes. You can even put a picture of your reward on your mirror to help motivate you.

Poor Mary had been wearing baggy sweat pants since I met her. All of her old clothes didn't fit properly and she didn't like the way they fit her. My suggestion to her was to buy a new pair of "skinny jeans" when she hit 25% body fat. And guess what, she did. Those jeans looked 'pretty darn awesome' on her!

10. MAKE IT PERMANENT

Your health and fitness should be one of your top priorities throughout life. I know that life can sometimes force you to put yourself on the back burner. However, you have to find ways to make sure your new health and fitness lifestyle is permanent. Find ways to make it fun and fresh. I recommend that you find an event to train for. Maybe it's a half (or full) marathon, a 100 mile bike ride, or a long hiking trip. When you have a reason to work out, it becomes easier to do.

After Mary hit her 25% bodyfat goal, she set her sights on a high adventure vacation with her daughter. 18 months after I met Mary, she went on a trip to Colorado and mountain biked more than 50 miles, white-water rafted and hiked some of the most beautiful trails that Colorado had to offer. Not bad for a lady who couldn't do one push-up when I met her. I now see Mary every 6-8 months, and I can't wait to hear what new adventure she has planned.

Are you ready to change your life through fitness? If you follow the same 10 steps that Mary did, you can enjoy the life-changing benefits. Maybe you can put on a pair of skinny jeans. Or you can walk up a few flights of stairs without gasping for air. Who knows, you may decide to run your first marathon. Whatever you want from your life, NOW is the time to go after it!

About Sean

Sean Millhouse is the head personal trainer and owner of Fitness 101. He is also a partner in Northwest Personal Training Center (Northwest Houston's largest Personal Training Facility). Sean and his businesses have helped more than 3500 clients meet their goals through the development of healthy fitness and eating habits.

Sean has been an ACE Certified Personal Trainer for 14 years and holds a Bachelor of Business Administration from the University of Houston - Downtown. Through ACE, he is also an Advanced Health and Fitness Specialist.

Through his multiple Personal Fitness Programs... Sean has worked with several local celebrities and successful business owners in the Northwest Houston area. His focus is on helping people who have lost control of their lives. Sean teaches that if we start practicing moderation, we can achieve balance and live a healthy lifestyle.

To help change lives through fitness...Sean offers his knowledge for lunch-and-learn opportunities, health and fitness seminars, and various charity functions.

Sean also publishes a Blog at: www.fitness-101.com and a weekly e-newsletter "Fit For Life" that help readers stay current with health and fitness topics. Archived articles are available on the blog.

For more information on Fitness 101's programs Visit their website at: www.fitness-101.com.

CHAPTER 11

Fitness is Not a FAD – It's Your Health Care

By John D. Eberley

Historically, fitness was the natural consequence of our basic survival needs. The life-long pursuit of food, clothing and shelter was more than enough physical activity to maintain a high level of fitness.

Prior to World War II, "exercising" was largely a fad in that it wasn't required for the average person to stay fit.

Since the Second World War, there have been massive changes. Perhaps the biggest changes have been the agricultural revolution and the development of modern food processing, which have forever changed our lifestyles. It didn't take us very long to recognize the benefits of these advances. Unfortunately, we're just beginning to understand the downside.

One of the unintended consequences of this abundant, yet sedentary lifestyle; has been the elimination of 'fitness by default.'

Today fitness is almost exclusively the direct result of focused physical activity more commonly referred to as EXERCISE. The amount of exercise individuals performed started to rise in the 1970's. Dr. Ken Cooper got everyone running and Arnold Schwarzenegger got them into the gym.

Since the mid-eighties however, exercise levels have plummeted to an all time low. Recent official reports state that only 15% of Canadians[1] and just 20% of Americans[2] meet their government's recommended guidelines for physical activity. It seems as though the average person has mistaken fitness for a fad.

Fad: an intense but short-lived fashion; a craze.[3] There have been all kinds of fitness fads, **but fitness itself is never a fad.**

The Centers for Disease Control (CDC) released a report stating that millions of Americans suffer needlessly from illnesses that can be prevented or improved through regular physical activity.[4]

Numbers Each Year	Exercise prevents or improves the risk of
95,000 are diagnosed with colon cancer	developing colon cancer
250,000 suffer a hip fractures	developing osteoporosis
1.5 million suffer a heart attack and 13.5 million have coronary heart disease	developing heart disease
8 million develop diabetes (type 2)	developing diabetes
50 million have high blood pressure	developing high blood pressure
Over 60 million are overweight	developing obesity or overweight

When an essential component of HEALTH is missing – fitness – what else would you expect?

The CDC report goes on to state that physical activity reduces feelings of depression and anxiety, while increasing the strength and co-ordination of the elderly.[4]

Is it any wonder that health care spending is out of control?

Which brings me to another point – don't expect any currently-practiced health care system (including the up-coming 'Obama Care') to offer any real help. Western medicine, also known as Allopathy, has proven to be a horrible form of health care.

Why? Quite simply, because it isn't health care – it's disease care.

> *"Learning is not compulsory, but neither is survival."*
> *- W. Edwards Deming,*

Canadians are particularly proud of their health care - and most believe it to be the best in the world. Health Canada's mission statement is,

"To maintain and improve the health of Canadians." A great **proactive** mission statement, unfortunately the western medical model of health care is **reactive**. It truly doesn't have a chance of meeting its stated mission.

Western medicine is a system based on disease care. Training focuses on disease identification and then intervention with pharmaceutical drugs and/or surgical procedures.

Most people don't even think of going to their doctor until their health has failed (infection, chronic pain, mood disorder, etc.). Western medicine is a reactive system whose expertise is in life or death situations.

Hey, when its life or death, western medicine can work miracles. If I've just been in a car accident and my face is lying on the floor, I want the best reconstructive surgeon, not a personal trainer!

These are services we absolutely need, but saving lives and health-promoting activities are two very different things.

The biggest problem is that the vast majority of people using the health care system – are not facing critical situations. They are afflicted with poor lifestyle habits – unhealthy diets, a lack of physical fitness and bad programming. These are issues outside the 'tool box' of western medical training.

When our health care system tries to manage lifestyle factors using drugs and surgery, the results are at best unpredictable, and at worst - death. I'm not exaggerating, below is a list published in the Journal of the American Medical Association (JAMA).[5]

Deaths Caused by Western Medicine
7,000 annual deaths from - Medical errors in hospitals
12,000 annual deaths from - Unnecessary surgeries
20,000 annual deaths from - Miscellaneous errors
80,000 annual deaths from - Nosocomial (hospital-acquired/caused) infections
106,000 annual deaths from - Pharmaceutical drugs (correctly administered)
Totaling 225,000 Unnecessary Deaths **Each Year**

"Reality is not what it seems to be. But what it IS..."
- Jon Rappoport

Another example of western medicine's inadequacy is highlighted by a look at Life Expectancy. Governments can brag all they want, but if their countries' overall ranking worldwide continues to drop, they can't keep claiming to have the best health care.

Life Expectancy Rankings[6]

Country	Overall Ranking 1950
Canada	8th (M=66.4 / F=70.9)
United States	7th (M=66.0 / F=71.9)

Country	Overall Ranking 1990
Canada	9th (M=74.0 / F=80.7)
United States	17th (M=72.1 / F=79.0)

Country	Overall Ranking 2008
Canada	14th (M=80.34 / F=83.81)
United States	45th (M=78.0 / F=81.13)

I'm a sports fan, but if my team has missed the playoffs for 58 years in a row, and I continue to say that my team is the best - you'd call me delusional!

> *"An ounce of prevention is worth a pound of cure."*
> *– Benjamin Franklin*

Sometimes it's hard to understand the issue, until you view it from a different perspective.

In 2004, the JAMA published a study that identified the actual causes of death for the year 2000. This was the first study of its kind where they identified what the actual causes of death were, not their symptomatic names (cancer, heart disease, etc.).[7]

The Top 3 Actual Causes of Death for the year 2000 were:

• Tobacco usage (435,000 deaths; 18.1% of total US deaths)

• Poor diet and physical inactivity (400,000 deaths; 16.6%)

• Alcohol consumption (85,000 deaths; 3.5%).

All causes of death were lifestyle choices. The bottom line is that – Lifestyle – is the single biggest factor when it comes to an individual's health. In consciously altering your lifestyle to restore or optimize your health, you are practicing **self-care**.

SELF CARE is the ONLY effective form of health care; and a big part of self care is to **consistently work on improving your fitness level**.

When it comes to fitness, you're either moving forward or you're going backwards – by design. The human body is truly amazing. If you aren't placing regular 'demands' on your body – through physical and mental effort – the body **will not** continue to support those functions.

This process is called Atrophy.

> Atrophy: a wasting, shrinking or degeneration of an organ or tissue due to malnutrition, poor blood circulation, loss of nerve supply, disuse, disease or hormonal changes.[8]

How fast does the degeneration start? Science has documented muscle wasting in as little as three days following immobilization of a limb.[9]

The connection between the nervous system and the muscles they control is also affected. In addition to structural changes in muscle tissue, researchers found there was a greater degree of strength loss compared to the amount of muscle loss.[10]

In essence, the body forgets how to properly utilize and coordinate muscle function as a direct result of **disuse**. These 'disuse' changes have been **extensively** studied during human spaceflight, bed rest, and aging.[11]

Another serious disuse 'side-effect' is the change to the body's metabolism. Simply put, the body decides to stop burning fat and instead prefers carbohydrate (sugar) as the primary fuel source. These changes have also been documented during human spaceflight, bed rest, and aging.[11]

These metabolic adaptations are also known as Metabolic Syndrome, and one of the first signs is an accumulation of fat. Not just the unattractive kind that ruins bikini season, but the internal kind of fat build-up that surrounds your internal organs and radically increases your risk of: [12]

• cardiovascular disease

- diabetes

- high cholesterol/triglycerides

- high blood pressure

- obesity

You would have to have a lot of brain atrophy *to not* see the link between a low fitness level and the primary causes of premature death in our society.

NOW IS THE TIME to change your thinking about fitness.

"Iron rusts from disuse; water loses its purity from stagnation...
even so does inaction sap the vigour of the mind."
- Leonardo da Vinci

In his amazing book, *SPARK: The Revolutionary New Science of Exercise and the Brain*, Dr. John Ratey states; "Building muscles and conditioning the heart and lungs are essentially side-effects. I often tell my patients that the point of exercise is to build and condition the brain."

SPARK goes on to explain how a group of proteins (brain-derived neurotrophic factor or BDNF) is produced and released as a direct result of physical activity. Without this protein, memorization cannot occur. In other words, your ability to learn is directly related to your level of exercise. But it goes much deeper than that, BDNF literally improves neural function, promotes growth of the nervous system and protects neurons and glial cells against cellular death.

Other research has used MRI's to validate the benefit of exercise on the brain. Individuals between the age of 55 and 80, who had fitness levels from 0-10, performed 1 mile walks and treadmill stress tests. Then 3D MRI scans were completed, tissue atrophy was identified in specific brain regions. The areas that showed the greatest atrophy *previously* associated with aging also showed the greatest benefit from exercise.[13]

Aside from the 'anti-aging' benefits, researchers also noted significantly better results when both cardiovascular and resistance training were performed.[13]

Muscles even make you smarter. In another study on cognitive function a thousand people (♀ and ♂) between 55 and 100 (average age 80) with normal memory had their strength tested in 9 different muscle groups. After four years, those with the greater overall muscle strength had significantly less cognitive decline. How much? Sixty one percent less decline compared to those who were the weakest in the group.[14]

"Do not let what you cannot do interfere with what you can do."
- John Wooden, Basketball Hall of Famer

It's Never Too Late – Age is not an excuse to abstain! Exercise provides health benefits for those 80 years and older.

In this study, the participants were inactive and some had health concerns such as coronary artery disease and arthritis. Riding a stationary bike or walking on a treadmill for just 20 minutes twice a week resulted in significant health improvements during the 6-month study. The exercise led to improvements in peak oxygen consumption (how well a person transports and uses oxygen during exercise), systolic blood pressure dropped and aerobic endurance improved.[15]

Inactivity leads to dis-ease, which becomes DISEASE
Forget the genetics bull****, want to know if you're really
at risk for disease?

Almost 20 years ago, the JAMA published a study by Dr. Kenneth Cooper, the man who got everyone running and talking about 'aerobics'. He followed 13,000 people (men and women) at his aerobics center in Dallas for fifteen years. This study was controlled for the known risk factors of age, blood pressure, cardiovascular condition, family history, insulin metabolism, personal health history and even smoking.[16]

The results documented that **ALL** forms and incidence of cancer were closely related to an overall lack of physical fitness. The risk of cancer increased 300% for those who were unfit.[16]

Even the risk of accidental death **was lower** for those who were physically fit.[16]

In a more recent study, researchers from the University of Buffalo discovered inactivity to be a greater risk of death than being overweight or obese.[17]

The 12 year study collected data including body measurements and physical activity of over 9000 men aged thirty-five to seventy-nine. "Consistently, physical inactivity was a better predictor of all-cause mortality than being overweight or obese."[17]

"Our findings confirm that, independent of other known risk factors, such as hypertension, high cholesterol and smoking, physical activity exerts positive health benefits independent of body weight... The benefit may derive from the fact that regular moderate physical activity, no matter how much you weigh, appears to stimulate the immune system, improve insulin sensitivity and increase bone density, among other positive effects..."[17]

Inactivity - is the single greatest risk for premature death that science has been able to document.

THE BOTTOM LINE - LIVE FIT OR DIE YOUNG!

I could write a whole book on this topic, one chapter doesn't even scratch the surface. Every single aspect of life improves for those who are fit.

This is the definition of fitness I use at my facility:

> **fitness (fit'ness):** the ability to live your daily life without compromising for routine (physical, emotional, mental or spiritual) challenges

Note it states **daily**, it isn't referring to life's great challenges, such as divorce or the death of a loved one – these situations will overwhelm. It is referring to your ability to NOT pull back from your daily existence. If you suffer from anxiety in social situations, or physically can't go play in the park with the kids, or you can't reach the top shelf due to shoulder pain; then you lack fitness by the definition.

Most people can't even imagine a life as described by this definition. How sad.

Everyone has the same 168 hours in a week. Based on approximates; sleep requires 56, work 40-50, watching TV/internet 34, eating 21, fitness 5, misc 2.

That's only five hours per week, a mere 3% of your weekly time to maintain and improve your overall fitness. Life simply gets easier when you are fit. **There is nothing else that will positively improve your health, wellness and quality of life so effectively.**

Exercise is the ONLY way to fitness. No drug or surgical procedure can give you fitness. Fitness prevents premature death and disability – a claim no medical system can equal.

Quit treating fitness as a fad and recognize it for what it is – your only true Health CARE system.

If you want to know your past, look into your present conditions.
If you want to know your future, look into your present actions.
- Chinese Proverb

*Only you have the **power** – are you going to **exercise** it?*

References

1) 'Statscan issues dismal report on Canadian's activity levels' Globe & Mail, January 19th, 2011

2) 'New CDC Report Says Many Americans Get No Exercise' ABC NEWS, February 16th, 2011

3) http://www.thefreedictionary.com/FAD

4) http://www.cdc.gov/nccdphp/sgr/mm.htm

5) Actual Causes of Death: Journal of the American Medical Association, Vol. 284, No. 4, July 28, 2000.

6) Life Expectancy Rankings

1950 American Journal of Clinical Nutrition, 1992; 55(Suppl):1196S

1990 American Journal of Clinical Nutrition, 1992; 55(Suppl):1196S

2008 Male numbers: http://www.infoplease.com/ipa/A0934746.html

2008 Female numbers: http://www.nationmaster.com/graph/hea_lif_exp_at_bir_fem-health-life-expectancy-birth-female&date=2008

*2008 Overall ranking based on male life expectancy, female numbers changed outcomes – some up, some down.

7) Journal of the American Medical Association, 2004; 291:1238-1245

8) Dictionary of Optometry and Visual Science, 7th edition, 2009 Butterworth-Heinemann

9) Lindboe CF, Platou CS. Effect of immobilization of short duration on the muscle fibre size. Clin Physiol 1984;4:183-188

10) Duchateau J, Hainaut K. Electrical and mechanical changes in immobilized human muscle. J Appl Physiol 1987;62:2168-2173.

11) J. Nutr. 135:1824S-1828S, July 2005

12) Archives of Internal Medicine May 24, 2004;164(10):1092-7

13) Journal of Gerontology: Medical Sciences, February 2003.

14) http://archneur.ama-assn.org/cgi/content/abstract/66/11/1339

15) Journal of the American Geriatrics Society December 2002; 50:2009-2013

16) Blair SN, et al. Journal of the American Medical Association, 1989; 262:2395-2401.

17) Annals of Epidemiology, Volume 12, Issue 8, November 2002, Pages 543–552.

About John

John D. Eberley has been active in the health and fitness field for thirty years. In his teens, John was a nationally ranked (amateur) bodybuilder. During this time he was fascinated by the ability to physically transform the body through exercise and diet. John noted how his adult gym peers were so much more physically active and younger, compared to 'other' adults of similar age. These early experiences set the stage for a keen understanding of the importance of FITNESS.

In 1987, John lost his mother to a three-year battle with cancer. This was by far the single biggest influence on the direction his life would take. His passion for "bodybuilding" shifted to fitness and identifying the lifestyles and behaviors that help or hinder human health, wellness and performance.

During the next decade, these insights were tested as John endured several personal challenges. John's renaissance came when he turned his focus and intensity towards uncovering the truth found in scientifically based research and natural laws. He then began applying this knowledge and insight to fitness, nutrition, stress-reduction, and recovery.

In January 2011, John introduced the culmination of his work (so far) with, **The "New" Health Care** paradigm at **FUSION- Human Development & Performance Corporation** in Calgary, Alberta. Pro athlete or 'all star' soccer mom - this unique approach and proprietary training methods help get their clients off the bench and back in the game.

As Founder and President of FUSION- Human Development & Performance Corporation, John continues to guide and inspire others in his revolutionary understanding of fitness, health and healing of the whole self.

For more information, visit: www.fusionhdp.com

CHAPTER 12

The 3-4-5 Total Body Fat Loss System

By Stephen Holt

"A more logical way of achieving fitness" – Baltimore Sun

It was the best news I'd ever heard...

We were pregnant (as we new millennium dads like to say)!

But my wife was a medical school resident while I had the typical personal trainer's schedule of working as early as 5:30 AM and as late as 9:00 PM. Surely, something had to change. And that "something" had to be my schedule, certainly not hers.

And what about my workouts? To a small degree, staying in shape is part of my business. But now, with a baby and a wife who was away every third night and recovering the next night (leaving just one "normal" day out of three), I needed to find a new way to get results in less time.

You see, most trainers spend most of their time in the gym, and when we're not working, we're working out. So it was easy to exercise 1½ to 2 hours a day, every day. And when you put in that kind of time, it's easy (or at least, easier) to get results.

Plus, you have more options (naps, massage - depending on your club, or simply enduring nearly debilitating soreness) than "normal" people to recover from strenuous workouts. Certainly I could no longer work so hard in the weight room that I was virtually worthless by the end of the day. I had to be fresh enough to meet the baby's needs at any time.

Years ago, one of the leaders in the field told me one of the best tips I ever learned: "Work out *only* as much as your clients do." But he was talking about a short-term experiment. Two to three weeks at most! I needed to come up with a long-range plan. I had to change my whole philosophy on fitness training.

I confess...my fitness background started with me "playing" football at Duke. I say "playing" in quotes because I wasn't good enough to do much actual playing at all. In order to compensate for a lack of talent, I studied strength and conditioning nearly as much as I studied engineering.

Consequently, I fell into the trap of training clients virtually the same way everyone else did – with the same bodybuilding principles we used in football. Sure, I'd studied more than any trainer I knew. I even spoke at national conventions and wrote for all the major trade magazines, but basically, I'd let the exercise equipment companies brainwash me.

After years of studying books and videos, and attending countless seminars and conventions, I finally combined my knowledge of fitness and anatomy with my Duke University mechanical engineering background, started thinking for myself and discovered **The 3-4-5 Total Body Fat Loss System**.

You see, the average program for the average person is based on bodybuilding lore – exercises that exist mainly because they have always existed. But one of the first things most of my clients say to me is, "I don't want to look like a bodybuilder." So why continue to train with exercises aimed at maximizing the size of a handful of individual muscles? And most of us aren't interested in living a bodybuilder's lifestyle. We don't have time to lift as long or as frequently as bodybuilders.

Your body has more than 600 muscles each connected to your bones in spiral and diagonal patterns, not in straight lines. Doesn't it make sense to acknowledge and respect these patterns in the exercises you do?

Most traditional exercises, however, assume a straight-line connection, and many standard machines actually force you to move in straight lines. We don't have time to do isolation exercises for every single muscle we can name – and even different heads of different muscles.

Think about it...how much time would you have to spend in the gym if you did an exercise for each head of the biceps, each head of the triceps, each head of the deltoids, each head of the quadriceps, etc. No wonder you feel like you spend all day at the gym and still don't get much done.

The answer is to completely change the way you look at exercise. No more isolation movements that try to work one muscle head at a time.

The answer is to incorporate moves that work as many muscles as possible. Remember, the more muscle mass you use, the more calories you'll burn. The answer is to work your muscles together the way they normally work everywhere but in the weight room.

My clients have reported outstanding fat loss, strength gains, and increased stamina using these techniques. More important, they have more fun, remain enthusiastic and just plain feel better – in addition to looking better.

The basis of the **"3-4-5 Total Body Fat Loss System"** is working:

I.   All **3** Planes of Motion

II. All **4** Major Muscle Systems (not the "major muscle groups" you've probably read about)

III. All **5** Fundamental Movement Patterns

Let's take a closer look at each of these...

I. 3 PLANES OF MOTION

The three planes of movement are the sagittal (front and back), frontal (side-to-side) and transverse (rotation).

A foundation of the "3" in the 3-4-5 system is that all muscles have some action in all three planes. So it makes sense to work in all three dimensions. Traditional bodybuilding exercises don't do that - not well, at least.

II. 4 MUSCLE SYSTEMS

Here's where it gets a little complicated, but bear with me for a moment. You only need to understand the concepts for now, not the details.

Recent research tells us certain muscles work together in four major "systems" (sometimes called "subsystems" or "sling systems") – don't let the fancy names throw you, though.

1. The **Anterior Oblique System (AOS)** connects your obliques and inner thigh muscles.

2. The **Posterior Oblique System (POS)** consists of your *latissimus dorsi* (lats) and *gluteus maximus* (glutes). The fibers of these two muscles also cross your sacroiliac (SI) joint and support this often troublesome spot.

   Since your glutes are the largest muscles in your body and your lats are the largest muscles in your the upper body, working this system is excellent for calorie burning.

3. The **Lateral System (LS)** consists of the "outer thigh" and inner thigh muscles of one leg, and the opposite *quadratus lumborum*, a muscle often implicated in low back pain.

   These muscles act to keep you upright whenever you're on one leg (as in walking).

   When you drive a car, for example, you're constantly

steering slightly to the left and slightly to the right to keep the car moving in a relatively straight line.

The same idea applies to your inner and outer thigh muscles. They work in unison to keep your hips relatively level and your knees facing relatively straight ahead as you move.

4. The **Deep Longitudinal System (DLS)** starts with a muscle connected to your big toe, goes up the side of your leg, and continues on to connect your hamstrings and the muscles along your spine. It's affected whenever your foot is on the ground and is a vital shock absorption system.

To get the most of out of your DLS and LS, and to burn the most calories, we'll do most of our exercises standing.

III. 5 FUNDAMENTAL MOVEMENT PATTERNS

Now it gets simple, again. We break down movement into five general patterns: pulling, pushing, rotation, one leg stance, and moving your center of gravity (COG).

(a). **Pulling exercises** (moving your hands toward your body – like a row) help fortify your POS, and strengthen your mid-back, low back and the dozens of muscles along your spine.

(b). **Pushing exercises** (moving your hands away from your body – like a chest press or shoulder press for simple examples) integrate your chest, shoulder and arm muscles with your abdominals, while your hips and legs stabilize.

Pushing or pulling exercises using just one arm also accentuate the way your obliques, spinal and mid-back muscles all work together in what's called "the serape effect."

(c). **Rotation exercises** emphasize your obliques and include the often neglected rotational function of many other muscles including your hamstrings and inner thigh muscles.

Your hips should have a large degree of rotation, yet no [commonly available] machine strengthens this movement. More important, many people have lost the rotation in their hips and shoulder girdle, so when they rotate -- as we do all day long – that rotation is focused in their spine. This is a common cause of low back pain.

Though they might appear harmful at first glance, standing rotational exercises can help restore hip and upper body rotation that can actually decrease the stress on your low back.

(d). **One leg stance**. Did you know that walking requires you to spend about 80 percent of your time on one leg or the other?

Exercises that combine a one-leg stance with your foot hitting the ground (lunges are prime example) teach your leg muscles to react subconsciously, to keep you upright.

(e). **Moving Your COG** (as in a squat, for example) works virtually all of your lower-body muscles in addition to your low back. COG exercises are great for teaching and reinforcing proper lifting mechanics and dynamic spinal stabilization.

PUTTING "3" "4" AND "5" TOGETHER

Now you can combine the "3" planes of movement, "4" outer unit systems and "5" basic movement patterns to make your workouts more efficient than ever before.

It's not nearly as complicated as it seems at first. Certain moves automatically fall into several groups at once. Any one-leg exercise automatically works your Lateral System and at least one plane. Any one-arm exercise for either the AOS or the POS will typically cover transverse plane and rotation.

So the 3-4-5 plan (combined with the results of the musculo-skeletal assessment) tells us which exercises to choose. Here's how we put it all together. We put the exercises together in what we call an "A/B" split, simply two different workouts.

We pair exercises so that you work in an "X" pattern. For example, an exercise emphasizing (remember, we're not isolating) the front of your upper body is followed by an exercise emphasizing the back of your lower body (a "hamstring-dominant exercise" in trainer jargon).

Upper body back ╲ ╱ Upper body front

Lower body back ╱ ╲ Lower body front

Now, this part is a little trickier, but stay with me...

The difference between your "A" workout and your "B" workout in this case would be that you'd do a 1-arm push exercise paired with a 2-leg hamstring dominant exercise in one workout. The next workout would pair a 2-arm push exercise with a 1-leg hamstring dominant exercise.

Here's what the template looks like:

Workout A
Strength

Workout B
Strength

2-Leg Ham. dominant	1-Leg Ham. dominant
1-Arm Push	2-Arm Push
1-Leg Knee dominant	2-Leg Knee dominant
2-Arm Pull	1-Arm Pull

And here's a more specific example using generic exercises

Workout A Strength	Workout B Strength
Kettlebell Swing	Single Leg Deadlift
1-Arm Push	Push Ups
Lunges	Squats
2-Arm Barbell Row	1-Arm Dumbbell Row

The workout starts with a **dynamic warm up** - what some trainers call "Movement Prep (Preparation)." This takes about 6-7 minutes and gets not just your muscles but also your nervous system ready for more intense work.

Next, we focus on **core training**. With most people, simply one exercise targeting the front of the body and one exercise targeting the back of the body is enough. This should take another 6-7 minutes. Plus, we pick strength training exercises that work your core even more. (14 minutes max, so far)

Then comes the strength-training segment. In most cases and in most workouts, we'll combine a total body power exercise with one of the templates you saw above so that you're doing a circuit of five exercises: power, upper, lower, upper, lower.

We go through the exercises with about 30-45 seconds of rest in between. The phrase we use is "comfortably uncomfortable." Three rounds of this circuit will take under 24 minutes. (38 minutes max, so far)

We add "finishers" to enhance fat burning even more. These types of exercises are hard (frankly) even when you're fresh and extremely hard at the end of a workout, but this technique has been scientifically proven to accelerate fat loss. We plan 4-6 minutes for these.

There, done in under 45 minutes!

Here's your **3-4-5 Total Body Fat Loss Workout** at a glance:

(i). Dynamic Warm-Up

(ii). Core Training
    2-3 rounds
    front core/back core

(iii). Strength Training
    5 exercise circuit
    power
    upper body - front
    lower body - back
    upper body - back
    lower body - front

(iv). Finisher

Getting started with the 3-4-5 Total Body Fat Loss System is really that simple. In addition to the 3,4,5 principles, your keys are to:

- use your legs in each exercise

- use some unilateral (one arm and/or one leg) exercises in each workout

- incorporate rotation when possible

With my **3-4-5 Total Body Fitness System**, you can work virtually all your muscles in a single, time-effective session while increasing calorie-burning during and - even more important - after the workout, building at least a little more muscle (which is a good thing), alleviating boredom, and avoiding plateaus – all at the same time.

Knowing that you only have to cover three simple rules of all three planes, all four muscle systems and all five movement patterns ensures that you strengthen every muscle in a way that builds—not ignores— the way muscles naturally work together.

At the same time, the flexibility of the **3-4-5 Total Body Fitness System** leaves much to your imagination, and keeps your workouts fun, exciting and productive.

About Stephen

Stephen Holt, "America's Baby Boomer Fitness Expert," is a best-selling author and nutrition and fitness expert who is regularly sought out by the media for his opinions on fat loss for busy moms. Stephen has been seen on NBC, CBS, and ABC affiliates as well as in *Shape, Woman's Day, Family Circle, Women's Health, Runner's World, Fitness*, and many more.

After over two decades of educating other personal trainers, Stephen went out on his own to found **29 Again Custom Fitness**, which in less than two years after opening, was named "Best of 2012 in Lutherville/Timonium - Health Club & Gyms Division" by the U.S. Commerce Association.

Stephen has been praised as "One of America's Greatest Trainers" by Men's Fitness and was named "Personal Trainer of the Year" by the American Council on Exercise following the national publication of his revolutionary and proprietary "3-4-5 Total Body Fat Loss System."

To learn more about Stephen Holt's **3-4-5 Total Body Fat Loss System** and grab your FREE Special Report, *"The 5 Supplements Women Need for Fat Loss Right Now,"* visit: www.facebook.com/StephenHoltFitness, or call: 410-429-7029.

CHAPTER 13

Training As We Age

By Bruce Kelly

For purposes of this chapter, we will first define what age group we are referring to as anyone over the age of 40. That may seem somewhat arbitrary but we have to start somewhere, right?

Now that we have that out of the way we will get to the heart of the matter and that is that our population is shifting to an older demographic as the Baby Boomers, a very large group, move into their 40's, 50's, 60's and beyond. And many of these Baby Boomers at least strive to stay active and eat well.

But the problem as I see it, is the huge amount of poor information this group gets on training as they age. Both the health care and the training community cater to the lowest common denominator when it comes to advising and working with this age group in my opinion.

Let me explain what I mean by that last statement by the use of an example:

Jack LaLanne was obviously an exemplar of fitness, eating well and doing extraordinary physical feats even as he moved into his 60's and 70's. But Jack LaLanne was also looked at as somewhat of a kook, an outlier, and even a freak. The fact of the matter is that LaLanne was a sickly, weak child and was never an elite athlete. But by mere dint of effort, working hard every day and being consistent in his training, he was able to maintain amazing physical capacity well into his 7th, 8th and even 9th decade. LaLanne should not be looked at as an outlier but as what a normal person can do if they put their mind to it.

But we have settled for the minimum based on things like studies that use sedentary subjects to draw their conclusions of what aging adults are capable of physically. Of course, we don't think aging people are capable of anything based on those premises! We have been taught that the detrimental impact of aging is inevitable and to just accept it. But it is now well known that this is absolute non-sense. That is just a self-fulfilling prophecy and there is plenty of evidence to prove it.

I am a still a competitive athlete and have been all of my life. And I see first hand evidence of what people can do in the autumn or winter of their lives. At the US Squash National Masters championships, they have an 80+ age division, which annually has 10-12 men in it. Softball, singles squash is the most demanding ball sport in the world, yet these great grandfathers are playing it very well. Likewise, at National and International Masters Track and Field or the National NASTAR (ski racing championships. The list goes on and on with the point being that most of these people weren't elite athletes when they were younger, but just people that either stayed active their entire lives or developed a passion for it in mid-life and were literally reborn.

I am not saying that everyone has to become a Masters athlete. What I am saying is that the physical decline of aging isn't inevitable but largely a matter of lifestyle choices. And don't for a moment think that there isn't a connection between physical aging/decline and diminished mental capacity. That link has been well established in books like *"Spark"* by Dr. Daniel Ratey.

So as a consequence the frequently recommended training regimen for our Baby Boomers goes something like this: machine-based strength training so as not to get "hurt" and long, steady-state cardio for conditioning and "fat loss." When will we come to our senses and realize that this is utter nonsense?

First of all, the last thing you need to do when you've likely been sitting at a desk all day is to go the your local gym and then sit some more to do your so-called strength training. If "sitting is the new smoking" as was recently cited in an Internet article, then why would your training entail even more sitting? That doesn't make any sense! Likewise with the so-called "cardio" that is frequently recommended for this group.

Two of the most popular forms of cardio training involve more sitting i.e. stationary cycling and rowing. Just what the doctor ordered after a day in front of a computer screen. Even a modicum of common sense would indicate that is not the way to go to improve someone's fitness and health – especially if done on a consistent basis.

We are not entirely beholden to our genetic make-up, either. Though genes do play a role in disease, our lifestyle choices largely determine whether those genetic predispositions, both good and bad, are activated or not. So don't use your parents as an excuse for why you're inactive, overweight and 'out of shape.' That is all on you!

There has to be a mindset shift that takes place in order to serve this Baby Boomer community better. This group needs more movement not less, and needs to do things that challenge them but are appropriate for their lifestyle, current health and fitness levels and schedules. I'm assuming most people that are reading this want to lead an active, robust life as they age, and not be confined by physical limitations that were largely of their own doing.

Here are some of my recommendations for what we could do to improve this situation:

- **Get assessed/evaluated first:** "If you ain't assessing, you're guessing." –Alwyn Cosgrove of Results Fitness in California, one of the most successful gyms in the U.S. His point is you have to have some baseline information on your fitness, strength, core strength, body comp., etc. to help determine where your program should start and what progressions are appropriate for you.

- **Develop a Plan:** There very few, if any, lay people that are truly qualified to put together a comprehensive, functional training program. And notice I said "training program."

The latest routine from Muscle and Fiction is not a training program. You can exercise or workout but the most efficient way to reach your goals is with a training program specifically designed with your goals in mind. That means appropriate levels of intensity and volume, safe progressions, and the capacity to be "tweaked" where necessary. That is where hiring a good trainer is worth every penny, in my opinion. You don't/shouldn't do your own taxes or serve as your own attorney. The most important asset you have, your health and fitness, should not be treated any differently.

- **Do Mobility Work Everyday:** Mobility is a broader, more practical concept of movement than flexibility. Mobility is the joint system's capability without external influence or force. Mobility incorporates flexibility. It also is a quality we can maintain well into older ages if we do something to work on it.

- **Do Soft Tissue Work Daily:** Whether this is done with Self Myofascial Release (SMR) through the use of tools like foam rollers, sticks and small balls or through self-massage or regular massage work is up to you. For most people, from a practical and a budgetary perspective, it will be a combination of these modalities. The point is that especially as we age things like trigger points and scar tissue develop, and you have to regularly work on trying to minimize their encroachment on your movement function or you will end up looking like Cro-Magnon man/woman!

- **Train Power:** We lose power at twice the rate we lose strength. A simple definition of power = force x speed/distance. So it has components of speed and force development. Many people mistakenly think that power training is only for athletes but what do you think is the key factor in fall prevention? Yes, power. Find ways to train it appropriately and safely for you. I would say sprint and jump if you can do it safely. If not, find what works for you.

• **Vary Your Energy System Development (ESD) work:** Don't get stuck in the rut of just doing long, steady-state "cardio." That is a never-ending cycle like a dog chasing its tail. It has value but it is not the Holy Grail of fitness that so many think it is. Do some interval, fartlek style training several times a week to add some variety and challenge to your ESD. You can incorporate that into running routines, biking routines, swimming, and even walking by doing more hills at a brisk pace. Or you can play an intermittent power sport like squash or soccer if you're ready for it. You won't be reading a book while doing that I assure you! ☺

• **Learn to "Chill":** It is now well researched and known about the benefits of stress reduction activities like meditation, deep breathing exercises, yoga and the like. Stress kills, quite simply, and has direct, measurable physiological impact on our health if we don't learn to manage it. So figure a way to get it into your schedule. Your mind/body will thank you for it, believe me!

• **Strength Train:** This is unequivocal. You must strength train and the sooner you start the better, but it is never too late. There is research out there that shows that even people in their 70's and 80's can benefit from strength training. It's benefits include, but are not limited to: improved balance, better bone health and bone mineral density, decreased rates of sarcopenia (muscle loss as we age), a key component of power development, strengthens connective tissue, and builds muscle/lean body mass(LBM). This last point is huge as nothing else will build LBM, period. It is only resistance training that will maintain your muscle and body composition.

And though this may ruffle some feathers, Yoga and Pilates aren't strength training, at least not in a comprehensive sense. I believe they have great value but let's not make them out to be a panacea for all that ails us.

- **Move More:** Think of the 10,000 step rule...try to get as close to that as possible each day. There is a concept called NEPA (Non-exercise Physical Activity) which could include things like gardening, walking the dog, taking the stairs instead of the elevator, house work, etc. The point is that those with higher levels of NEPA tend to be fitter, leaner and have better overall health. It only makes sense...we are meant to move and there is no pill that will ever change that fact!

- **Improve Your Nutrition:** There is a saying we use in my training facility: "You can't out-train bad nutrition." I didn't coin the term, but whoever did knew what they were talking about, that much is certain. You can train 3-4 hours a day but if you eat poorly, it will all be for nothing. A basic philosophy is to eat close to the Earth: if it doesn't have a Mother or come from the Earth then don't eat it. That means Doritos and French fries don't meet those criteria. And on the supplement question, if your diet isn't very clean 90% of the time, you are fooling yourself and wasting your money to think supplements will "solve" a poor diet.

- **Be Consistent:** The worst training program in the world if done consistently will out-perform the best training program if done sporadically. The body must be put under training stress (there is good stress as well) repeatedly and consistently in order for training adaptations to take place. That is why a little each day is better than a lot every 10 days.

- **Train both Sides of Your Body:** This is especially true for men who, if left to their own devices, would train just their biceps, chest and abs. If effective, this results in a top heavy, front-loaded, bird-leg look that is an aesthetic and functional disaster. It plays havoc with your posture, can lead to low back issues and robs you of your movement skills and athleticism. Women are usually slightly better but have been brainwashed by years of infomercials and other nonsense that convince them they will "bulk up" if they lift heavy weights...there is no science to back up such a claim, but it persists nonetheless. Women should train similarly to men (after all we are the same species, I believe!) although probably will not use loads as heavy as men but loads appropriate for them. Remember **Strong is the New Skinny**.

• **Push Yourself:** Obviously, this has to be appropriate for your age, condition and history, but I believe we are too often told to "take it easy" as we age when it comes to things physical. Why? Again, it feeds into that self-fulfilling prophecy of diminished expectations which lead to worse outcomes. You aren't/won't be what you were physically in your 20's, at least if you weren't a total slug at that time. But we always relish challenges, I believe, so don't be afraid to try new things or push the envelope, where appropriate and safe, every once in a while. It will energize and rejuvenate you.

• **Incorporate Variety:** For most of us, we will get bored if we do one or several things all of the time to the exclusion of most everything else. So add variety to your routine and avoid boredom and staleness. That doesn't mean you don't need consistency in your foundational modes of movement/ exercise, but doing new and different things is one of the reasons you want to prolong your physical functionality in the first place. If you're on vacation, you want to do that snorkeling excursion, try sea kayaking, hike that trail, or go on that all-day guided tour of a great, historic city.

• **Have Fun:** I can't define what that is for everyone, but the point is that you will more likely stay with physical activities that you enjoy. Whether that is cycling, dancing, swimming, Pilates, racquet sports, Yoga, or strength training is really not the issue. You will do it if you like it. But bear in mind that no mode of exercise/movement is a be all, end all, comprehensive way to functional capacity – no matter what the zealots of various exercise "cults" may tell you. So though you may have your favorite(s) unless they are covering all of the components of functional fitness, you will have to supplement them in some way to cover those gaps.

So I hope these tips help you get started on your journey to improving your functional capacity and fitness. We have the technology, drugs and medical science now to extend life but at what cost to one's soul and spirit? We can live full, active lives well into our 80's and perhaps beyond if we do the right things now and going forward: move every day and eat well.

The choice is yours!☺

About Bruce

Bruce L. Kelly, MS, CSCS has nearly 30 years coaching/ training experience working with a wide spectrum of clients from desk jockeys to a number of collegiate athletes in a variety of sports.

Coach Kelly has worked in a variety of training settings from "Big Box" mega gyms to smaller facilities. For the last 6 years, he has owned/operated his own training facility in Media, Pa. (outside of Philadelphia) – Kelly High Performance Training/Fitness Together Media.

At KHPT, Coach Kelly and his staff of 6 implement their "functional" training system using movement-based training to help people feel better, look better and perform better. Their two primary training population niches are middle school, high school and collegiate athletes, and "Baby Boomers."

Coach Kelly has a MS in Exercise Science (Concentration in Performance Enhancement and Injury Prevention) and a large number of nationally recognized certifications including:

- NSCA-CSCS, NSCA-CPT

- NASM-PES (Performance Enhancement Specialist)

- FMS - Level 1 & 2 Certified

- TPI - Level 1 Certified

- USATF - Level 2 Sprints/Hurdles/Jumps

- Precision Nutrition - Level 1 certified

- KB Athletics - Level 1

- Maxwell S&C Kettlebell - Level 1

Coach Kelly contributes frequently to Mike Boyle's strengthcoach.com website on a number of topics. He also has two blogs: http://kellyfitnessrants.blogspot. com/ and http://kellystrainingmastersathletes.blogspot.com/

Coach Kelly's contact information is: http://fitnesstogether.com/media and brucekelly@fitnesstogether.com

CHAPTER 14

How To Look Better Naked

By Ryan Toth

I have been a personal trainer for 8 years and have had countless clients come to me saying they want to train with me to get into shape, to lose weight, or to get healthy. Those are all great reasons to work with a trainer, but, let's face it folks, the real reason anyone is willing to go kill themselves at the gym is this – they want to look better naked!

Don't get me wrong, getting healthy is definitely part of the plan, but real results come when you can visualize your progress every day. Transforming your body into the sleek machine you *want* to see in the mirror takes work, and an *accountability blueprint* makes building the "perfect you" attainable.

What is an accountability blueprint? As with any other blueprint, your accountability blueprint will map out every step you need to take to construct the new you. You cannot build something new if you keep returning to the same, comfortable lies. We all lie to ourselves; it's a fact. We tell ourselves "I deserve this meal; I worked hard" or "I will start my diet plan on Monday." Get over this: you do not deserve to eat anything you want just because you worked out or because you had a rough day. You do not deserve that last meal prior to starting your weight loss plan! What you deserve is the chance to be honest with yourself and to achieve your goals.

I have a client named Melissa, who won our most recent transformations contest. She is a working mom with two kids who never knows what end is up! Originally, she participated in a weight loss contest and *gained* weight. (This is more common than you realize.) You can imagine her frustration! We had to sit down when she began the contest a second time, and have a frank chat. I asked her, "Are you ready for this?" If you cannot commit, you will not succeed. Melissa's second try was a huge success – she lost 30 lbs and six dress sizes in 12 weeks! She won our contest because she was ready and prepared for the challenge, and she had an accountability blueprint just like the one you will build for yourself after reading this chapter.

ARE YOU READY?

No fitness plan will work for you if you aren't ready for the process. This is going to be work, so you had better be ready in spirit, mind, and body to follow your plan and attain your goals. Did you just change jobs, are really stressed, and working sixty-hour weeks? Are you in the middle of a major life change such as buying a house or having a baby? It is better to tackle only one life-altering event at a time. If you think you aren't mentally ready to commit to a long-term plan just now, you might want to consider postponing the start of your makeover program. If that is the case, try changing only one element at a time such as altering only your nutritional plan so that you don't become overwhelmed and 'throw in the towel' in two weeks.

CREATING YOUR ACCOUNTABILITY BLUEPRINT

If you are ready for real change, step one in creating your plan is to find out *why* you want to create the plan in the first place. Be honest with yourself. Do you want to wear a smaller dress size for your sister's wedding? Are you dreading that you will attend your 20th high school reunion and people will see you as you currently are – 50 lbs. overweight? Dig deep. Is your self-esteem shot because you don't feel or look the way you think you should? If all else fails, just admit that you really want to look better naked. Whatever your reason, own it. Your "why" is what will get you through the process. The beginnings and endings of the plan are obvious; the "why" will get you through the difficult parts in the middle.

For step two of your accountability blueprint, you will create a check-in sheet for yourself with points earned for each item you can check off that day. You can assign as many points as you wish for each item on the check sheet. For example, weighing yourself only once daily will gain you 5 points. You must also decide how many points you will lose if you miss some of the key points on your checklist!

Some items on your checklist should include:

• Weigh yourself no more than one time per day.

• Eat five meals a day that contain a protein and a vegetable.

• Eat NO SNACKS. Calories add up. Snacks don't exist.
  If you are eating then it must be a meal.

• Workout every day for at least 20 minutes.

• Allow 20 minutes per day for self-reflection.

• Sleep seven or more hours per night. More sleep equals greater time for your body to recover plus more fat burning power.

• Limit alcoholic beverages to 1 per week.

• Drink 3 liters of water daily.

• Track your food intake daily. Be honest about what you are eating.

SET A TIMELINE

Set a goal for a maximum of twelve weeks at a time. For example, if you want to lose two dress sizes in 12 weeks for the wedding you will be attending, that means you need to lose one dress size every six weeks. A dress size equals 3" in the waist lost in 6 weeks or ½" from your waist per week. You can easily lose ½" per week!

Set mini-goals for yourself. Any large-scale project can be overwhelming if all you see is the finish product you need to have but no plan of attack. Losing 15 lbs. seems an insurmountable task – until you realize that is only 1¼ lbs a week.

PLAN FOR SUCCESS

If you aren't a math person, you might find it difficult to compute how many calories you need to cut from your daily intake to achieve 1¼ lbs a week. Plan for your own success by utilizing any of the many computer or phone apps to help you track your calorie intake, including how many fewer per day you will need to achieve success. Plan your meals. You should eat five meals per day consisting of at least a protein and a vegetable. Pre-cook your food and portion it out with a scale for accuracy. Establish the times when you will eat your meals. It will be far easier to feel a little bit hungry now if you know there is only an hour until your next meal. Eating on a schedule will keep your blood sugar in check and your energy levels consistent. Trust me; I work 18-hour days too and can still make this eating plan work.

ANNOUNCE YOUR GOAL

Accountability to others keeps you on track, and friends and family can be great motivators. Announce your goal to the world. Once you have put it out there, you will be far less likely to renege on your promises to yourself. No one wants to be a quitter or a failure. Use social media to your advantage; if you already tweet or update your Facebook status regularly, use those forums to let people know your progress.

FIND OR CREATE A SUPPORT GROUP

Even with a plan, there are bound to be challenges that knock you off track. You need access to a support group to help you work through your challenges and get back on the wagon. Being part of a group with the same goal as yours increases your chance of success. If you have a family, enlist their help in your success. They can cheer you on and cheer you up.

You generally want at least three people in your support group. This ensures that if any one of the people in your group is also having a rough spot and having a hard time being supportive, at least one other person likely can still be there to cheer you on.

There are two types of accountability: workout accountability and nutritional accountability. The key is to get them BOTH on the same page. Your friends need to be able to tell you, "Hey, you are screwing up!" Every week, everyone in the support group provides feedback to each other member.

What have been your successes and what have been your failures? You must be able to admit where you are failing. You cannot drop some food off your nutritional list and not admit that you are consuming those calories; they still exist.

What if you aren't good at working with groups? You ask. If face-to-face meetings with other people trying to get in shape unnerve you, you might try an email group. Alternatively, are you one of those people who don't want to listen to anyone else? If you are one of those people who is not ready right now to account to a group – or maybe you have never been a team player – then you need to keep a journal and be brutally honest with yourself. Keep photos in your journal. Track your food. You will probably be surprised what you are really eating. When are you eating? Why are you CHOOSING to eat at this time?

JOURNALING

Everyone should keep a journal to chronicle his transformation. Your journal begins with your assessment of your readiness, your goal and your "why" for embarking on this exciting mission. You can track your food in your journal, how much you ate, and why you chose certain foods. Knowing what feelings trigger certain eating patterns can assist you in staying on track. Once you know that stress sends you rummaging through the pantry, then overcoming your stress should quickly involve a change of scenery or a walk to get away from the pantry.

Use your journal to hold yourself accountable for each element on your checklist. If you aren't making it to the gym or exercising for 20 minutes daily, why aren't you? A frank conversation with yourself could tell you that you think Zumba is boring. Do something different.

TAKE PICTURES

No, you do not have to take pictures of yourself naked to see the results. For women I recommend wearing a sports bra and shorts. Men should wear shorts and no shirt. Take a picture of yourself every two weeks. The camera doesn't lie; it is an excellent way to track the changes, or lack of them, on your body. Keep these photos with you and near you: hang one from the fridge, place one in the pantry, keep one on the dashboard of your car, and put one in your purse or wallet. Document your fitness journey the same way you would document the other milestones of your life.

REFLECTION

The final component you will add to your accountability blueprint is reflection time. You deserve twenty minutes of reflection or meditation time each day. Reflection is your chance to just be in the moment and focus on you without distraction. Go in a quiet room – your car if you have to—and think. You will be devoting many hours on working your plan and holding yourself accountable, so a few minutes processing what you are learning about yourself while following your accountability blueprint is the time to recharge your batteries.

Before you race off to create your own blueprint, here are a few additional pointers. Sample one of the wonderful available Apps to help you track your progress. Three good Apps are: My Fitness Pal, Daily Plate, and Livestrong, but there are many others. Adopt the new food motto "if it can't expire; don't eat it." Moreover, if your waist needs whittling, avoid grains, nitrates and anything artificial.

If you are not sure that you need a fitness accountability blueprint, I challenge you to really take a good look in the mirror. Kudos if you love what you see! If you want to become healthier, lose weight or just look better naked, today is your day. You now have the tools to create your own accountability blueprint. Go for it.

About Ryan

"Work hard, have fun, get sexy!" That's New Jersey Personal Trainer Ryan Toth's personal motto – and the central theme of his popular Total Core Fitness Boot Camp programs.

Ryan grew up in Central New Jersey, where he was the quarterback of the Metuchen High School football team. He attended college at Kean University, playing 2 years of college football, before graduating with a B.A. in communications.

Ryan Toth's true passion, however, was fitness – so he continued his education by studying for and receiving his certification as a personal trainer. He was especially interested in the boot camp fitness concept of bringing diverse groups of people together for intense, challenging workouts that were also unpredictable and fun. He approached a local YMCA and convinced them to let him start a boot camp program, and it wound up being such a huge success that many people joined the Y just to get into the camp.

His growing reputation and devoted fan base allowed Toth to launch his own business, Total Core Fitness Boot Camp. There, he began offering fun, high intensity workouts, a manageable class size of just 15 "campers," and a very affordable rate.

After five years of steady growth, the program has expanded to two locations, in Metuchen and Sayreville. Additionally, for those times when his "campers" can't make it to a class, Toth created the At Home Transformation Bootcamp, which he makes available for FREE on his website: www.totalcorefitcamp. com. The program is comprised of a series of exercises that can be done anywhere, using only a chair, and has been featured on local TV.

Ryan is married to his very understanding wife, Dori, who he met in high school. They have three children – five-year-old Evan, three-year-old Ryan and Caitlyn, four months old.

CHAPTER 15

Reduce Stress And Improve Your Health

By Matt Luxton

Let me tell you the story of a recent client, Grant, to help illustrate a few simple processes that will have dramatic impacts on all aspects of your health. Grant came to my studio one Thursday afternoon after work. His head was spinning like a roulette table, and he explained to me that he had a 'to-do' list that looked more like a Christmas food shopping list.

He was overwhelmed, and he didn't really know where to start. Grant drank alcohol at the end of work, found himself making poor food choices, his joints ached, he was heavier than ever and he was getting stressed about getting stressed!

It was time to take action.

Before I lay out the exact strategies that I used with Grant its worth noting that within 6 weeks his blood pressure went from hypertensive to almost optimal, he lost 18 lbs of body fat, 22 inches around his body including 6 off his waist. It didn't stop here; he continued to lose fat in the remaining 6 weeks of his programme and lost over 2 stone (28 lbs.). Oh, and in that time Grant bought a house, entered a triathlon and continued to run his own business. So I didn't lock him in solitary confinement to get the results!!

The first step is to reduce stress. A stressed body is unlikely to lose body fat and keep it off. Stress comes in many forms and is very well illustrated by Seth Godin, author of The Dip, with his stress bucket. This very simply illustrates that stress comes in various forms and if you continue to fill up your bucket, you will eventually overflow resulting in a relapse and sickness.

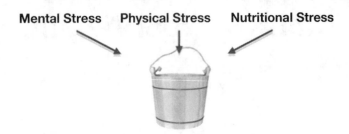

Simply adding the strategies below, without removing certain stress-ors, is likely to increase stress. For example adding high intensity training to your already excessive training volume is not optimal; it is much like adding supplements to a poor diet.

THE THREE TIERED APPROACH TO REDUCING STRESS & IMPROVING HEALTH

I. Reduce & Remove

Remove before you add! What do I mean, often people want to jump straight in to their latest goal, training every day or adding time to each session. Unfortunately, if you don't remove stress first, you will be running with the brakes on. Removing stressors is not just about nutrition, its not all about lifestyle, its not just reducing or adding exercise, it's a more holistic approach and an integration of efficient and proven principles, rather than chasing the latest fad.

II. Support

By adding a few specific principle-based approaches to your life, you too can experience dramatically improved quality of life and daily function.

III. Challenge

Once you have got these systems in place you are ready to attack any challenge that life may throw at you. Whether it is a daily chore that used to wear you out or that 'thing' you have been meaning to do for years, now you are ready!

I. REDUCE NUTRITIONAL STRESS

Clean, Whole, Naturally-Sourced – The Way Things Should Have Been

I am an advocate of the Elimination style of nutrition. I was first introduced to this approach by my mentor and coach Dax Moy. In a nutshell (no pun intended), this system removes known or suspected sources of intolerance. Many of the most common illnesses and pathologies could be reduced if not eradicated by using such simple protocols. Sure this is not the only nutritional strategy that works, but for me it lies comfortably within my philosophy of what food should be about.

• **Remove stressors and toxins – including sugar.**

Knowing that something is potentially harmful or detrimental to your health, you would think that it wouldn't be in our daily foods right? However, not all food companies and producers care about their customers, they are really interested in the number of packets they sell! One of the biggest fallacies that still seem to be lurking is the 'low fat' con! If you take a look at the back of the packet, there's a fair chance that this product is very high in sugars. Sugar is one of the leading causes of obesity and data from the National Health and Nutrition Examination Survey in America shows that since 1980, obesity prevalence among children and adolescents has almost tripled.

Sugar comes in natural forms in fruit and in milk and also in added forms. There are many pseudonyms that these hide under. A study conducted by the American Diabetes Association (2012) found that those people who had high fructose levels in their diets also had high levels of the dangerous visceral fat that surrounds their vital organs. It is worth noting here that overall weight is not always linked to fructose consumption, confirming that you can be a 'skinny-fat' person. This is someone who doesn't obviously carry huge excess body fat, but on the inside they are not healthy. This is more dangerous than carrying the sub-cutaneous fat that looks unsightly but doesn't carry the same risks in illness and disease.

[Greater Fructose Consumption Is Associated with Cardiometabolic Risk Markers and Visceral Adiposity in Adolescents. J. Nutr. 2012 142: 2 251-257; first published online December 21, 2011]

• **Supportive nutrition.**

Now, whilst we would all love to get everything we need from our food, unfortunately due to the soil quality and methods of farming we cannot always guarantee the quality of our foods when they arrive at our door. To improve this, we can buy as local and fresh as possible and try to eat organically to avoid the pesticides that have a massive effect on our thyroid and ultimately our body's ability to burn calories at rest.

There are only five (5) supplements that I would recommend taking without meeting you, but as always consult your doctor before thinking of improving your nutrition or exercise habits.

1. Milk Thistle.

2. Magnesium

3. Zinc

4. A good quality Fish oil.

5. Tulsi tea

When all is said and done there is nothing like keeping it simple. A quote that I love is one by Ralph Waldo Emerson, which sums it up in one hit, "As to methods, there may be a million and then some, but principles are few. The man who grasps principles can successfully select his own methods. The man who tries methods, ignoring principles, is sure to have trouble." So, just by sticking with a few principles you can see how you too can avoid the latest fad.

• **Alkalise.**

Having excessively acidic conditions in your body is one of the major causes of impaired fat loss and illness. Acidic conditions cause increases in cortisol and impaired function of other hormones that regulate fat loss. Processed foods are the ones you need to avoid. The green leafy and cruciferous vegetables are among the best at optimising blood sugars and reducing acidity. The fruits that buck the trend are avocado and tomatoes. Almonds and brazil nuts (unsalted and not laced in chocolate of course) are two great sources of good fats that are both alkaline, along with pumpkin seeds, sunflower seeds and flax seed oil.

II. EXERCISE

• **Efficient.**

Now in case you missed a lot of recent trials and experiments, High Intensity Interval Training (H.I.I.T) is now getting the recognition it deserves. For too long people have been taking part in inefficient, time-intensive training, when they could have achieved better results in less time. It goes without saying that you should arrange a health check with your GP before starting any new exercise regime, but a really simple protocol that I like to use with my clientele to help improve blood pressure is to combine one upper body exercise with one lower body. This is known as blood shunting and reduces total peripheral resistance to blood flow by opening up all the arteries and capillaries around the body.

• **Dynamic.**

After a long day sitting at a desk or in your car, the last thing you want to be doing is to be seated at a gym, confined by the dimensions of another generically-designed machine that will do nothing for the way you move, feel and perform. My simple instructions to you here are to seek exercises that use as many joints as possible, and also mimic the movement patterns that you want to improve on. This may be as simple as posture or as complex as sports performance, either way get out of the machine and use the best tool you have, your own body.

• **Supportive.**

Supportive exercises are essential for improving your weaknesses. In our contemporary lifestyles, with much of it spent seated, we are all prone to certain movement dysfuntions. A lot of them manifest themselves in a forward head posture and an excessive kyphotic (upper back) and lordotic (lower back) curve. Tight or overactive quadriceps inhibit, arguably, the most important muscles for performance and fat loss, the glutes (buttocks)! My advice here is not necessarily to self-diagnose, but to be aware that working on the muscles that are on the back of your body will often help alleviate some of the common problems caused by contemporary living styles. What I did with Grant was to use two pulling exercises for every one pushing exercise to help address this. We also focused on hip-dominant exercises to help activate lazy glutes as a result of his sedentary lifestyle and occupation.

III. LIFESTYLE

I put this at the end, not because it's the least important, but because it's the bit that needs the most attention in most clients that I meet.

1. Sleep

Clients like Grant often ask me for advice, complaining of waking too often, feeling like they didn't get a wink, or struggling to get off to sleep.

Sleep is crucial for producing the Human Growth Hormone (HGH), required to repair cells, aid brain function, increase enzyme production and improve bone strength. HGH is mostly produced during the early hours of sleep (between 10pm and 2am), hence why getting to bed by 10pm most nights of the week is so important. Shippen and Fryer (2007) attributed the decreased speed of healing and brain function, in middle age, to a decline in the production of repair hormones.

Locking your front door will increase your sense of security and enhance your chances of relaxing sleep. You have to shut down all social media sites at least 30 minutes before bed. It only takes one person's status update to affect your sleep.

2. Being aware of your social circles.

Try to surround yourself with positive and proactive people. Its not always possible, but you can to a large extent dictate with whom you spend your quality time. Avoiding 'sappers' as Clive Woodward (World Cup Winning England Rugby Coach) calls them, is essential if you want to feel good and create an environment of which you look forward to being a part. If your goals mean something to you, which they should do, share them with five people today. Why? Because this creates accountability and the more people who know when, what and why you want to achieve it, the more likely you are to achieve it. So go on, share it with your social circle, it's powerful stuff!

3. Creating Win/Win situations.

When I first came across this I was reading a book by Stephen Covey, The 7 Habits of Highly Effective People. This book helped me to understand that if I could help more people get things they wanted, I would in turn create happiness in my life. What's really important here is that your goals are not to the detriment of those around you (Win/Lose). Often, when I speak with parents, I find they have spent too long prioritising others to the detriment of their own well-being. This is not about being entirely selfish, but you need to create situations more often than not where everyone is a winner.

For example, Grant asked his wife for 40 minutes 3-5 times per week so that he could exercise, and in return he took his two young children out for one afternoon each weekend to give his partner a break. A really simple one, but you can see how both partners are winning here.

4. Create Clarity and Consistency

Do you ever get that feeling that you are spinning plates, juggling your daily tasks? I did too, but now I spend a lot more time doing the things I enjoy and have created priorities in and around my weekly schedule.

The first thing I did was to draw a table on a white board. This acted as my 'to-do' list but it was in 4 quarters. Much like the diagram below.

This helped me to concentrate on the things that really needed doing versus the tasks that weren't urgent or important. Give it a go, it's very

	URGENT	NOT URGENT
IMPORTANT	• crises • pressing problems • deadline e-driven projects, meetings, preparations	• preparation • prevention • values clarification • planning • relationship building • true recreation • empowermnt
NOT IMPORTANT	• interruptions, some phone calls • some mail, some reports • some meetings • many proximate, pressing matters • many popular activities	• trivia, busy work • some phone calls • "escape" activities • irrelevant mail • excessive TV

rewarding. To give you an example at this present moment, I have writing this chapter in the top left quadrant along with the preparation run for my half marathon and hanging out my washing in the bottom right.

This is one that you should definitely do if you are busy. Stop the mundane tasks running your life! To give you an example, I only do banking on Fridays, I only pay bills on Tuesdays and I only do washing on a Thursday and Saturday morning. Those are just three examples of how I limit busy-ness in my life and in the lives of my clients.

Create clarity in all areas of your life, starting with your goals. Just by simply knowing what you want and writing it down you will be far more likely to achieve it. Start by qualifying your goal, so if it is weight-related, then say how much and how many inches off your waist. Then start to understand what is necessary to achieve it. I often refer to this as the 'metaphorical price' you need to pay to achieve it. How many sessions do you need to do, how many hours sleep do you need or which foods needed to be added to your nutritional plan?

Next, the most successful clients are the ones who educate themselves, by reading around their chosen goal. This is one of the key principles in my mission statement, which empowers clients to make healthy decisions long after our time together. The excitement this creates can be phenomenal and I experienced this first hand last year when I completed the trek to Machu Picchu. Learning about this was almost as good as the trek itself, so you can imagine how excited I was when I got there.

With your goals you should then try to keep them in your conscious mind, and keep asking yourself what it will mean to you or what it will feel like. If this doesn't get you excited then you either need to change the outcome, or change the way in which you intend to get there. Now it's time to test your goal and find out what your first action will be.

Creating this kind of excitement around your goal is so powerful and it doesn't always just have to be in fitness but in all areas of your life. It is fantastic. So go on, start plotting your journey by following the aforementioned steps.

I am excited for you.

About Matt

Matt Luxton, also known as 'The Functional Training Specialist,' is a health and fitness expert that is regularly sought after by his communities both in his home region in the South West of the United Kingdom and online for his systems that really work when it comes to health, fitness and fat loss.

Matt is the founder of Functionally Aware Fitness Personal Training Studios, creator of the Hot to Trot Nutritional Plan and author of *The Equestrian Athlete Plan and Hot to Trot Cookbook*. Matt has written articles for his readers through paper and magazine articles. Matt is known for his holistic approach to health that places his clientele's long-term wellbeing as paramount with fitness and fat loss a natural occurrence through his training systems.

Matt founded FA Fitness Personal Training back in 2008 and since then has gone on to create the Blast Fat Loss Formula. This has manifested itself in the Blast Fat Loss Mentorship, a 28-Day Online programme that empowers clients to make health based decisions for the rest of their lives.

To learn more about Matt and his Blast Training Systems, please head to: www.fa-fitness.co.uk – where you can receive the FREE special report *The 7 Sins of Fat Loss*.

CHAPTER 16

The Spirit Of Training

By George Cormack

A Polarizing Story

Last week, a woman came in and wanted to join the "Biggest Loser" competition at my gym, the U2 Fitness Centre.

"Why?" I responded.

"I need to lose weight," she answered, in a matter-of-fact sort of way.

"Okay, but *why* do you want to lose the weight?" I asked again.

"I just want to lose the weight!" she said, seemingly annoyed at all the questions. That was not good enough. I don't take people who can't tell me why they want to lose the weight.

"The doctor told me to lose the weight," she said, still trying.

"Well, do *you* want to lose the weight?" I asked.

"I have to," she quickly responded. She still did not understand why I was asking these simple, yet probing questions. I told her that it was about wanting to lose the weight. No one *has* to do anything. It takes a desire, especially in the fitness world, to accomplish any goals.

Her final effort was her spelling out all the ailments that had come on, because of her excess weight. "The doctors told me I need to reduce my blood pressure, and I am going to have diabetes," she added.

I asked her one more time why she wanted to lose the weight? I honestly didn't care what the doctors told her.

"Well…" she started to say.

I stopped her right there. I answered for her, and told her that she, in fact, didn't want to lose the weight. She wanted someone else to lose it for her. I sent her home, but I told her all was not lost. Once she could commit and apply a good spirit to this effort, then I would take her on.

On the other side of the spectrum, I had another woman come in, who said she too wanted to join the "Biggest Loser" competition.

"Okay, why?" I asked her.

"I'm fat, I'm ugly, I hate myself, and I want to change!" she quickly responded, without even thinking. "I need help!"

"Come on down!" I said. "Tell me more." She told me about her family life, and what she had been doing to help other people. She had gotten so caught up in everyone else, she had forgotten about herself.

She knew it was her time now, as well as how much weight she wanted to lose. She realized it was going to be hard, and wanted guidance on what else she could do to make it happen. This is the type of client that gives me goose bumps. My final questions, to finish assessing her spirit, were what her worst and best things she had ever done. Her worst was burying her mother. Her best …

"I think I'm doing it now," she said. Wow, is all I can say! She may have been broken, hurting, and crying inside, but she was ready for a change.

That's two women – the same age and weight: one looking for us to lose the weight for her, the other crying out for our help.

How do we connect with that? How do we change the lives of these women? It's sitting down and listening. God gave us two ears and one tongue. We have to listen for a person's spirit first, then let them know what we are going to do.

Out of 100 people that sign up for a gym membership, left on their own, 70 won't come into the gym or may only come in a few times at best. Now, out of the remaining 30, around half will use the gym on a regular basis. These are the people that are self-motivated.

This is where the motivation came from to look at this lack of a spirit in training. We shouldn't just have gym memberships; we should have "training memberships." You come in for a specific reason. You come in to lose weight, tone your body, bulk up, or even rehabilitation. You come in for a reason! Those are the people I want to work with. Those are people ready to work.

What is a membership? Why do I have to have a membership? We have been blinded as fitness professionals that we need to sell these memberships. Why? A membership is nothing. It is either a piece of paper or your name in the computer. You need to be moved, be trained.

We need to get the connection right with the people. I reflect back to my Biblical studies. It was easier for Jesus to train his 12 disciples, who whole-heartedly believed in him. When he tried to train the masses, they turned on him. We need to do the same thing, and train our staff to work with people, not just take a membership.

How do we get that specialized training that actually works? We have to listen to our clients at first, not the other way around. We need to understand them before we instruct them. I see a lot of gyms, where the trainers take over and bulldoze the clients. They don't listen.

MY WAY OF TRAINING

I try to teach people that I'm their coach, not their backbone. As you can see from the woman I sent home, I want to empower clients, not do the work for them. That creates an independence, which means they control their own destiny. What better feeling in life is there than to have control of your own life?

To achieve this, you have to understand what's required of you. You need to have a positive spirit and strong effort. No one is going to do it for you, and I'm a big believer in taking charge of your own destiny.

We, as humans, have a lot of support mechanisms. Use them to grow, but be careful not to use them too much and stunt growth. I have been there too. I know when I went through my dark pain I had a lot of people supporting me. Their spirit allowed me to grow, like I'll allow you to grow, but I'm not going to do it for you!

WHAT IS THE SPIRIT OF TRAINING?

Jesus was training people from a very early age. He provided himself with 12 disciples to go out and spread the word. I like to train people to spread the word that your physical fitness and your spiritual fitness go hand in hand.

I remember an old horse trainer telling me, "Never break the spirit of the horse. Break him in and train him, but don't break his spirit, because you will have a horse that won't do anything."

Most people walk into gyms with broken spirits and do nothing. Their spirit is gone from abusive relationships, drugs, or even alcohol. They come in, and they are defeated in many ways.

Many run from training. We, as trainers, fail to invoke the spirit within them. The fear of change is enormous and can be paralyzing. How can I cope with change? Will I like myself when I change? These questions and others hold those people back, to the extent they fail to grow.

Oh no, did I say, "grow"? That means I have to grow up and be a big boy or girl. "Yes, why be fat and ugly? Just be ugly," I joke.

Get rid of the negative. Find the power within to rise up. Being knocked down in a fight is one thing, but do you stay down or get up. Most fighters get up, and the fight goes on. Life is a fight in many ways. We get knocked down. We get up and live to fight again. Being knocked down is not the end of the world, but staying down can be.

My father used to say, "You can't do it!" I would grit my teeth, and then show I could do it. I've made mistakes, but to this day, I'm still learning.

My brother is the polar opposite. We are very much like the two women discussed at the beginning of the chapter. My brother when he was told he couldn't do it, he wouldn't do it. He didn't make too many mistakes, but he didn't accomplish too much either. Our spirits are different – "Can Do" and "Don't Do."

Don't ever let the fear of failure hold you back from accomplishing great things!

My spirit enables me to conquer challenges that I never thought possible. "Accept the challenge, ride through the storm, and do great things," is a motto that I live by.

A FEW TIPS TO INVIGORATE THE SPIRIT

1. **Find a place where you can be at peace.** Use this place to focus on yourself, reflect, restore, and re-energize your mind. Channel good thoughts and love yourself.

2. **Appreciate what you have, not what you don't.** Say, "Thank you!" more for the air you breathe, the water you drink, the food you eat, the clothes on your back, and the fact you can actually exercise.

3. **Give yourself compliments and compliment someone else.** Give a smile, and see how you feel when that smile comes back to you. Wow, that is so powerful!

4. **Always reach higher.** It's foolish to limit yourself, and you can always obtain a higher mark. There are no records that can't be broken.

5. **Make the feeling of exercise yours.** It's an amazing thing to say, "I've done it!" Do it for yourself, no one else.

6. **Start your day with quiet time.** Read your goals and start new ones. Also, take this time to reflect or pray. Get the right spirit in your heart and mind for the challenges ahead.

GETTING PAST THE PLATEAU

One of the questions I hear the most is, "My spirits are always high at the beginning. I am seeing results and feel great. Then, these results start to slow. What do I do then?"

When you are going through a plateau, or your results are slowing a bit, what do you need?

Encouragement – You need to know you are okay, you are admired, and that you are doing well. You have support. You have good people all around you, so use this resource to get you through these tough times. When the chips are down, that's when your support should pick you back up!

Remember, you are rising up and heading toward a slimmer you. You are leaving that fat behind. We reinforce that, and the emphasis is just love yourself.

Pluses – Also, this is a good time to get your "pluses" going. During this time, the best thing to do is to get yourself thinking in a positive light again. You've come into the gym, you gotten off your couch, and you even opened up to me to tell me you're feeling this plateau. That's five pluses already today.

If it's a Monday and you're feeling down, I want you to get 25 pluses by Friday night. Then, come in and tell me about your pluses. Allowing those pluses to happen is your good spirit. Focus on the positive, not the negative. There are no minuses in my gym.

REACHING YOUR GOALS, WHAT'S NEXT?

You've just lost 20 pounds. What now? I don't focus on just one goal, and I don't allow my clients to focus on just weight.

Numerous components contribute to weight loss. There's the exercise, the diet, the water they drink, and what's happening in their lives. *These are perennial goals that you must maintain for life!*

So what, you've lost 20 pounds? What about the other goals? This is about life, not just the weight. This is life-changing stuff we're talking about.

You said you wanted to see your family after you lost the weight. Great, what are they going to say when they see you? How are you going to feel?

Don't go over there and brag, but go over there and love that family more than ever. These are things that we still need to work on.

We all see the people that bulk up. They've gained 20 pounds, and they walk around like Arnold Schwarzenegger. Are you going to show those muscles off, or are they going to help you develop your character better?

Now, with that bigger body, how about sharing with someone else and helping them change?

That's training people with the right spirit. Once you start looking beyond yourself, the results just magnify.

A PERSONAL NOTE

Bob Dylan sang a song, "The Times They Are a-Changin'." Time never changes though, as we all have the same 24 hours. Things are changing around us, because we have become less active over the last 40 years.

So much is said about nutrition. We forget about exercise. More than 50 years ago, we didn't have TV. We didn't have computers or mobile phones. We actually walked, we rode bikes, and we climbed trees. We went outside. We didn't just sit on our butts. There is less labor-intensive work today, and people are sitting more. This creates a negative spirit to provide excuses.

Don't give me excuses, and don't ever say, "I can't!" Let's create a positive spirit, and let's get our butts moving!

For more information about the U2 Fitness Centre, visit: www.u2fitness.com.au.

About George

George Cormack is the CEO and head trainer of the U2 Fitness Centre in Warrnambool, Australia. George is known for his no-nonsense approach to training clients. George trains people to not only lose weight, but also to change their lifestyles. His passion for exercise has seen him take on challenges against much younger opponents, yet come away successful almost every time. At the age of 59, he is still able to keep his fitness age at 19.

George grew up in Scotland, the eldest of four sons. He was educated in the public system, but school was not really a focus in his life. His home life took center stage, as his father was a brutal man, who demanded fear of him, whether right or wrong was being done. George is the definition of perseverance, as he does not let anything from his childhood hinder his ability to help others now.

George's love for fitness came from necessity. His passion started with running. (In his younger days, running from fear of attack.) In school, the battle between the Catholics and Protestants was prominent. "I still carry those visible scars from attacks, not to mention the emotional scars," he honestly admits.

George played competitive soccer, hockey, and badminton. In his Young Farmers days, he excelled to become the Young Farmer of the Year in 1971. George moved to Australia in 1974, to work on a 20,000-acre property and play competitive soccer. He quickly became a force in the soccer world in Australia — playing, coaching, and promoting the game. His success led to regular radio, TV, and writing for newspapers.

George's life has had many twists and turns, but with his determination and strong focus to keep the road ahead clear, he has succeeded in having a major impact in people's lives. He became a fitness professional out of need, but has been no less dedicated. His health issues, with an Acoustic Neuroma, led him to take care of his body more than ever. Being a father of four children, he knew he had to be the breadwinner. He worked long hours, trained hard, and loved hard.

When his marriage to the mother of his children fell apart, George sought and found a close relationship with God. To this day, that unfettered relationship provides him with unlimited energy to serve his clients and children alike. "You are never alone when you have Jesus in your life," he proudly says.